Spring Data

Implement JPA repositories with less code and harness the performance of Redis in your applications

Petri Kainulainen

[PACKT] open source *
PUBLISHING
community experience distilled

BIRMINGHAM - MUMBAI

Spring Data

First published: November 2012

Production Reference: 2291012

Published by Packt Publishing Ltd.
Livery Place
35 Livery Street
Birmingham B3 2PB, UK.

ISBN 978-1-84951-904-5

www.packtpub.com

Cover Image by Abhishek Pandey (abhishek.pandey1210@gmail.com)

Credits

Author
Petri Kainulainen

Reviewers
Antti Koivisto

Jari Timonen

Timo Westkämper

Acquisition Editor
Usha Iyer

Commissioning Editor
Priyanka Shah

Technical Editor
Jalasha D'costa

Project Coordinator
Shraddha Bagadia

Proofreader
Maria Gould

Indexer
Hemangini Bari

Graphics
Aditi Gajjar

Production Coordinator
Arvindkumar Gupta

Cover Work
Arvindkumar Gupta

About the Author

Petri Kainulainen is a software developer living in Tampere, Finland. He is specialized in application development with the Java programming language and the Spring framework. Petri has over 10 years of experience in software development, and during his career he has participated in the development projects of Finland's leading online market places as a software architect. He is currently working at Vincit Oy as a passionate software developer.

I would like to thank my employer Vincit Oy for providing me with an endless supply of printer paper and an inspiring work environment that encouraged me to accept this challenge.

Writing this book would not have been possible without the help of my reviewers. I would like to thank Antti Koivisto, Jari Timonen, and Timo Westkämper for their comments and improvement ideas.

Finally, I would like to thank my family and friends for their support and encouragement. I am especially grateful to my mom and dad who bought me my first computer as a Christmas present when I was eight years old. Without this present, I would have probably chosen another profession and I would have never written this book.

About the Reviewers

Antti Koivisto is a Java EE architect, data transfer system specialist, data modeler, continuous delivery enthusiast, and a TDD practitioner. Antti has worked on all layers of n-tier web applications, all the way from the Linux server administration to jQuery and Search Engine Optimization (SEO). His weapons of choice come from SpringSource and his philosophy of "convention over configuration" comes from Ruby on Rails. Currently Antti works at Alma Mediapartners on the largest classified ad sites of Finland: `Etuovi.com` and `Autotalli.com`. Antti goes by `@koantweet` on Twitter.

Jari Timonen is an experienced software enthusiast with over 10 years of experience in the software industry. His experience includes successful team leadership combined with understanding complex business domains and delivering them into practice. Jari has been building enterprise architectures, designing software, and programming. While he started his career in the finance industry, he currently works as a Solution Architect in a telecommunications company. He practices pair programming and is keen on studying new technologies. When he is not building software, he is spending time with his family, fishing, or flying his radio controlled model helicopter.

Jari currently owns following certifications: Sun Certified Programmer for the Java 2 Platform, Standard Edition 5 (SCJP), Sun Certified Developer for the Java 2 Platform (SCJD), and Oracle Certified Master, Java EE 5 Enterprise Architect (OCMJEA).

Timo Westkämper is a Software Architect working at Java Enterprise consulting in the capital region of Finland. He has been working with Java technologies since 2004 and is especially interested in DSLs, query languages, and new languages for the JVM platform.

He is also the co-founder of Mysema and the maintainer of the popular querying library QueryDSL, which is tightly integrated into the Spring Data framework.

www.PacktPub.com

Support files, eBooks, discount offers and more

You might want to visit www.PacktPub.com for support files and downloads related to your book.

Did you know that Packt offers eBook versions of every book published, with PDF and ePub files available? You can upgrade to the eBook version at www.PacktPub.com and as a print book customer, you are entitled to a discount on the eBook copy. Get in touch with us at service@packtpub.com for more details.

At www.PacktPub.com, you can also read a collection of free technical articles, sign up for a range of free newsletters and receive exclusive discounts and offers on Packt books and eBooks.

http://PacktLib.PacktPub.com

Do you need instant solutions to your IT questions? PacktLib is Packt's online digital book library. Here, you can access, read and search across Packt's entire library of books.

Why Subscribe?

- Fully searchable across every book published by Packt
- Copy and paste, print and bookmark content
- On demand and accessible via web browser

Free Access for Packt account holders

If you have an account with Packt at www.PacktPub.com, you can use this to access PacktLib today and view nine entirely free books. Simply use your login credentials for immediate access.

Table of Contents

Preface   **1**

Chapter 1: Getting Started   **7**

  Java Persistence API   **8**

    Key concepts   9

    Creating database queries   9

      Native SQL queries   10

      Java Persistence Query Language   11

      The Criteria API   12

  Redis   **13**

    Supported data types   13

    Persistence   14

    Replication   15

    Publish/subscribe messaging pattern   15

  Summary   **16**

Chapter 2: Getting Started with Spring Data JPA   **17**

  Downloading dependencies with Maven   **17**

  Configuring the Spring application context   **19**

    Creating the properties file   19

    Creating the application context configuration class   20

      Creating the application context configuration skeleton   20

      Configuring the data source bean   21

      Configuring the entity manager factory bean   22

      Configuring the transaction manager bean   23

  Loading the application context configuration   **23**

  Implementing CRUD functionality for an entity   **24**

    Domain model   24

      Contact   25

      Address   28

    Creating a custom repository   30

      Creating a custom repository in the old school way   30

Creating a custom repository with Spring Data JPA	35
CRUD	**36**
Create	37
Read	38
Update	39
Delete	40
Summary	**40**
Chapter 3: Building Queries with Spring Data JPA	**41**
Building queries	**42**
Query methods	42
Query generation from method name	42
Named queries	46
@Query annotation	49
JPA Criteria API	52
Adding the JPA Criteria API support to a repository	52
Creating the criteria query	52
Creating the service method	54
Pros and cons	55
Querydsl	55
Configuring Querydsl-Maven integration	56
Generating Querydsl query types	57
Adding Querydsl support to a repository	58
Creating the executed query	58
Executing the created query	59
Pros and cons	59
What technique should we use?	60
Sorting query results	**60**
Sorting with method name	61
Creating the query method	61
Modifying the service method	61
Sorting with query strings	62
JPQL queries	62
SQL queries	62
Sorting with the Sort class	62
JpaRepository	63
Query generation from the method name	64
@Query annotation	64
JPA Criteria API	65
Sorting with Querydsl	65
What technique should we use?	67
Paginating query results	**67**
Changing the service layer	68
Creating a class for pagination parameters	68
Changing the service interface	69
Creating PageRequest objects	69

Implementing pagination	70
JpaRepository	70
Query generation from the method name	71
Named queries	71
@Query annotation	72
JPA Criteria API	74
Querydsl	74
Summary	**75**
Chapter 4: Adding Custom Functionality to JPA Repositories	**77**
Adding custom functionality to a single repository	**78**
Creating the custom interface	79
Implementing the created interface	79
Configuring the repository class	80
Implementing the custom methods	81
Creating the repository interface	82
Creating the service implementation	83
What did we just do?	83
Adding custom functionality to all repositories	**84**
Creating the base repository interface	84
Implementing the base repository interface	85
Creating the repository factory bean	86
Creating the skeleton of the repository factory bean class	86
Creating the repository factory inner class	86
Creating the builder method for the repository factory	88
Configuring Spring Data JPA	88
Creating the repository interface	88
Implementing the service layer	89
What did we just do?	89
Summary	**90**
Chapter 5: Getting Started with Spring Data Redis	**91**
Installing Redis	**92**
Getting the required dependencies	**94**
Configuring the Spring application context	**94**
Configuring the Redis connection	**95**
Configuring the Jedis connector	97
Configuring the JRedis connector	98
Configuring the RJC connector	99
Configuring the SRP connector	101
Summary	**102**
Chapter 6: Building Applications with Spring Data Redis	**103**
Designing a Redis data model	**104**
Key components	**105**

Atomic counters   105
RedisTemplate   105
  Operations   105
  Serializers   106
Implementing a CRUD application   **107**
Using default serializers   108
  Configuring the application context   108
  CRUD   109
Storing data in JSON   117
  Configuring the application context   117
  CRUD   118
The publish/subscribe messaging pattern   **123**
Creating message listeners   123
  Implementing the MessageListener interface   123
  Creating a POJO message listener   124
Configuring the application context   125
  Configuring the message listener beans   125
  Configuring the message listener adapter bean   125
  Configuring the message listener container bean   126
Sending messages with RedisTemplate   127
  Create   127
  Update   127
  Delete   128
Verifying the wanted behaviour   128
Using Spring cache abstraction with Spring Data Redis   **129**
Configuring the Spring cache abstraction   130
  Enabling caching annotations   130
  Configuring the host and port of the used Redis instance   131
  Configuring the Redis connection factory bean   131
  Configuring the Redis template bean   131
  Configuring the cache manager bean   132
Identifying the cached methods   132
  Adding contact information to the cache   133
  Updating the contact information to the cache   133
  Deleting contact information from the cache   133
Verifying that the Spring cache abstraction is working   134
Summary   **134**
Index   **135**

Preface

Spring Framework has always had good support for different data access technologies. However, one thing remained the same for a long period of time: developers had to implement their data access layer by using technology specific APIs, and often these APIs were not very concise. This led to a situation where one had to write a lot of boilerplate code in order to achieve the desired results. Sounds familiar, right?

The Spring Data project was born as an answer to these problems. Its goal is to provide an easier way to create applications, which use either relational databases or newer data access technologies such as non-relational databases, map-reduce frameworks, or cloud based storage technologies, with the Spring framework. It is essentially a parent project that collects data storage specific subprojects under a single brand. A full list of its subprojects can be found from the homepage of the Spring Data Project: http://www.springsource.org/spring-data/.

This book concentrates on two specific subprojects: Spring Data JPA and Spring Data Redis. You will learn an easier way to manage your entities and to create database queries with Spring Data JPA. This book also demonstrates how you can add custom functions to your repositories. You will also learn how you can use the Redis key-value store as data storage and to use its other features for the purpose of enhancing the performance of your applications.

This practical guide proves that implementing JPA repositories can be fun and helps you to harness the performance of Redis in your applications.

What this book covers

Chapter 1, Getting Started, gives a brief introduction to the technologies described in this book. This chapter is divided in two parts: the first part describes the motivation behind the Java Persistence API, outlines its main concepts, and shows how you can use it for building database queries. The second part identifies the key features of the Redis key-value store.

Chapter 2, Getting Started with Spring Data JPA, helps you to start building applications by using Spring Data JPA. You will learn to set up a project that uses Spring Data JPA and configure your application by using programmatic configuration. You will also learn an easy way to create repositories for your entities and implement a simple contact manager application by using Spring Data JPA.

Chapter 3, Building Queries with Spring Data JPA, describes the techniques that you can use to build database queries. After reading this chapter, you will know how to build database queries by using query methods, JPA Criteria API, and Querydsl. You will also continue the implementation of your contact manager application by adding a search function to it.

Chapter 4, Adding Custom Functionality to JPA Repositories, teaches you how you can customize your repositories. You will learn how you can add custom functionalities either to a single repository or to all repositories. The principles discussed in this chapter are demonstrated by customizing the repositories of your contact manager application.

Chapter 5, Getting Started with Spring Data Redis, will guide you through the installation and configuration phase that is required before you can use Spring Data Redis in your applications. It describes how you can install Redis to a computer running a Unix-like operating system. Then you can set up a project that uses Spring Data Redis. In the last part of this chapter, you will learn to configure the Redis connection and compare the features of the supported connector libraries.

Chapter 6, Building Applications with Spring Data Redis, teaches you how you can use Redis in your Spring powered applications. It describes the key components of Spring Data Redis and teaches you how to use them. You will also see Spring Data Redis in action when you use Redis as data storage of your contact manager application. The last part of this chapter describes how you can use Spring Data Redis as an implementation of the Spring 3.1 cache abstraction. You will also see how to utilize Redis' publish/subscribe messaging pattern implementation in this chapter.

What you need for this book

In order to run the code examples of this book, you will need to install the following software:

- Java 1.6
- Maven 3.0.X
- Redis 2.6.0-rc6
- A web browser

If you want to experiment with the code examples, you will also need:

- An IDE such as Eclipse, Netbeans, or IntelliJ Idea
- The full source code package for each chapter (See the following *Downloading the example code* section)

Who this book is for

This book is great for developers who are working with Spring-powered applications, and are looking for an easier way to write data access code that uses relational databases. Also, if you are interested in learning how you can utilize Redis in your applications, this is the book for you. This book assumes that you have got some experience from the Spring Framework and the Java Persistence API. No previous experience from Redis is required.

Conventions

In this book, you will find a number of styles of text that distinguish between different kinds of information. Here are some examples of these styles, and an explanation of their meaning.

Code words in text are shown as follows: "We can do this by using the `repositoryFactoryBeanClass` property of the `@EnableJpaRepositories` annotation."

A block of code is set as follows:

```
@Override
protected RepositoryFactorySupport createRepositoryFactory(EntityManag
er entityManager) {
    return new BaseRepositoryFactory(entityManager);
}
```

When we wish to draw your attention to a particular part of a code block, the relevant lines or items are set in bold:

```
@CachePut(value = "contacts", key="#p0.id")
@Transactional(rollbackFor = NotFoundException.class)
@Override
public Contact update(ContactDTO updated) throws NotFoundException {
    //Implementation remains unchanged.
}
```

New terms and **important words** are shown in bold.

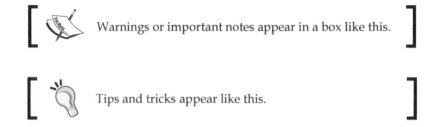

Warnings or important notes appear in a box like this.

Tips and tricks appear like this.

Reader feedback

Feedback from our readers is always welcome. Let us know what you think about this book—what you liked or may have disliked. Reader feedback is important for us to develop titles that you really get the most out of.

To send us general feedback, simply send an e-mail to feedback@packtpub.com, and mention the book title through the subject of your message.

If there is a topic that you have expertise in and you are interested in either writing or contributing to a book, see our author guide on www.packtpub.com/authors.

Customer support

Now that you are the proud owner of a Packt book, we have a number of things to help you to get the most from your purchase.

Downloading the example code

You can download the example code files for all Packt books you have purchased from your account at http://www.packtpub.com. If you purchased this book elsewhere, you can visit http://www.packtpub.com/support and register to have the files e-mailed directly to you.

Errata

Although we have taken every care to ensure the accuracy of our content, mistakes do happen. If you find a mistake in one of our books—maybe a mistake in the text or the code—we would be grateful if you would report this to us. By doing so, you can save other readers from frustration and help us improve subsequent versions of this book. If you find any errata, please report them by visiting http://www.packtpub.com/support, selecting your book, clicking on the **errata submission form** link, and entering the details of your errata. Once your errata are verified, your submission will be accepted and the errata will be uploaded to our website, or added to any list of existing errata, under the Errata section of that title.

Piracy

Piracy of copyright material on the Internet is an ongoing problem across all media. At Packt, we take the protection of our copyright and licenses very seriously. If you come across any illegal copies of our works, in any form, on the Internet, please provide us with the location address or website name immediately so that we can pursue a remedy.

Please contact us at copyright@packtpub.com with a link to the suspected pirated material.

We appreciate your help in protecting our authors, and our ability to bring you valuable content.

Questions

You can contact us at questions@packtpub.com if you are having a problem with any aspect of the book, and we will do our best to address it.

1
Getting Started

In this book, we will concentrate on two specific subprojects that offer support for Java Persistence API 2.0 and the Redis key-value store. But before we get to the point, we need to get a brief introduction to both the technologies. We need to do this for two reasons:

First, if we want to truly understand the benefits of Spring Data JPA, we need to have an idea on how database queries are created when the standard API is used. As soon as we compare these code samples to a query creation code that uses Spring Data JPA, its benefits are revealed to us.

Second, the basic knowledge about the Redis key-value store will help us to understand the second part of this book which describes how we can use it in our applications. After all, we should be familiar with any technology that we use in our applications. Right?

In this chapter, we will cover the following topics:

- The motivation behind the Java Persistence API
- The main components of the Java Persistence API
- How we can create database queries with the Java Persistence API
- The data types supported by the Redis key-value store.
- The main features of the Redis key-value store.

Java Persistence API

Before the **Java Persistence API** (**JPA**) was introduced, we had the following three alternative technologies which we could use to implement our persistence layer:

- The persistence mechanism provided by **Enterprise JavaBeans** (**EJB**) 2.x specifications
- The **JDBC** API
- The third party **object-relational mapping** (**ORM**) frameworks such as Hibernate.

This gave us some freedom when selecting the best tool for the job but as always, none of these options were problem free.

The problem with EJB 2.x was that it was too heavyweight and complicated. Its configuration relied on complicated XML documents and its programming model required a lot of boilerplate code. Also, EJB required that the application be deployed to a **Java EE** application server.

Programming against the JDBC API was rather simple and we could deploy our application in any servlet container. However, we had to write a lot of boilerplate code that was needed when we were transforming the information of our domain model to queries or building domain model objects from query results.

Third party ORM frameworks were often a good choice because they freed us from writing the unnecessary code that was used to build queries or to construct domain objects from query results. This freedom came with a price tag: objects and relational data are not compatible creatures, and even though ORM frameworks can solve most of the problems caused by the **object-relational mismatch**, the problems that they cannot solve efficiently are the ones that cause us the most pain.

The Java Persistence API provides a standard mechanism for implementing a persistence layer that uses relational databases. Its main motivation was to replace the persistence mechanism of EJB 2.x and to provide a standardized approach for object-relational mapping. Many of its features were originally introduced by the third party ORM frameworks, which have later become implementations of the Java Persistence API. The following section introduces its key concepts and describes how we can create queries with it.

Key concepts

An **entity** is a persistent domain object. Each **entity class** generally represents a single database table, and an instance of such a class contains the data of a single table row. Each entity instance always has a unique object identifier, which is the same thing to an entity that a primary key is to a database table.

An **entity manager factory** creates **entity manager** instances. All entity manager instances created by the same entity manager factory will use the same configuration and database. If you need to access multiple databases, you must configure one entity manager factory per used database. The methods of the entity manager factory are specified by the `EntityManagerFactory` interface.

The entity manager manages the entities of the application. The entity manager can be used to perform **CRUD** (**Create**, **Read**, **Updated**, and **Delete**) operations on entities and run complex queries against a database. The methods of an entity manager are declared by the `EntityManager` interface.

A **persistence unit** specifies all entity classes, which are managed by the entity managers of the application. Each persistence unit contains all classes representing the data stored in a single database.

A **persistence context** contains entity instances. Inside a persistence context, there must be only one entity instance for each object identifier. Each persistence context is associated with a specific entity manager that manages the lifecycle of the entity instances contained by the persistence context.

Creating database queries

The Java Persistence API introduced two new methods for creating database queries: **Java Persistence Query Language** (JPQL) and the **Criteria API**. The queries written by using these technologies do not deal directly with database tables. Instead, queries are written over the entities of the application and their persistent state. This ensures, in theory, that the created queries are portable and not tied to a specific database schema or database provider.

It is also possible to use SQL queries, but this ties the application to a specific database schema. If database provider specific extensions are used, our application is tied to the database provider as well.

Next we will take a look at how we can use the Java Persistence API to build database queries by using SQL, JPQL, and the Criteria API. Our example query will fetch all contacts whose first name is "John" from the database. This example uses a simple entity class called `Contact` that represents the data stored in the `contacts` table. The following table maps the entity's properties to the columns of the database:

Contact	contacts
firstName	first_name

Native SQL queries

SQL is a standardized query language that is designed to manage data that is stored in relational databases. The following code example describes how we can implement the specified query by using SQL:

```
//Obtain an instance of the entity manager
EntityManager em = …

//Build the SQL query string with a query parameter
String getByFirstName="SELECT * FROM contacts c WHERE c.first_name =
?1";

//Create the Query instance
Query query = em.createNativeQuery(getByFirstName, Contact.class);

//Set the value of the query parameter
query.setParameter(1, "John");

//Get the list of results
List contacts = query.getResultList();
```

This example teaches us three things:

- We don't have to learn a new query language in order to build queries with JPA.
- The created query is not type safe and we must cast the results before we can use them.
- We have to run the application before we can verify our query for spelling or syntactical errors. This increases the length of the developer feedback loop and decreases productivity.

Because SQL queries are tied to a specific database schema (or to the used database provider), we should use them only when it is absolutely necessary. Often the reason for using SQL queries is performance, but we might also have other reasons for using it. For example, we might be migrating a legacy application to JPA and we don't have time to do it right at the beginning.

Java Persistence Query Language

JPQL is a string-based query language with a syntax resembling that of SQL. Thus, learning JPQL is fairly easy as long as you have some experience with SQL. The code example that executes the specified query is as follows:

```
//Obtain an instance of the entity manager
EntityManager em = …

//Build the JPQL query string with named parameter
String getByFirstName="SELECT c FROM Contact c WHERE c.firstName =
:firstName";

//Create the Query instance
TypedQuery<Contact> query = em.createQuery(getByFirstName, Contact.
class);

//Set the value of the named parameter
query.setParameter("firstName", "John");

//Get the list of results
List<Contact> contacts = query.getResultList();
```

This example tells us three things:

- The created query is type safe and we don't have to cast the query results.
- The JPQL query strings are very readable and easy to interpret.
- The created query strings cannot be verified during compilation. The only way to verify our query strings for spelling or syntactical errors is to run our application. Unfortunately, this means that the length of the developer feedback loop is increased, which decreases productivity.

JPQL is a good choice for static queries. In other words, if the number of query parameters is always the same, JPQL should be our weapon of choice. But implementing dynamic queries with JPQL is often cumbersome as we have to build the query string manually.

The Criteria API

The Criteria API was introduced to address the problems found while using JPQL and to standardize the criteria efforts of third party ORM frameworks. It is used to construct query definition objects, which are transformed to the executed SQL query. The next code example demonstrates that we can implement our query by using the Criteria API:

```
//Obtain an instance of entity manager
EntityManager em = …
//Get criteria builder
CriteriaBuilder cb = em.getCriteriaBuilder();

//Create criteria query
CriteriaQuery<Contact> query = cb.greateQuery(Contact.class);

//Create query root
Root<Contact> root = query.from(Contact.class);

//Create condition for the first name by using static meta
//model. You can also use "firstName" here.
Predicate firstNameIs = cb.equal(root.get(Contact_.firstName, "John");

//Specify the where condition of query
query.where(firstNameIs);

//Create typed query and get results
TypedQuery<Contact> q = em.createQuery(query);
List<Contact> contacts = q.getResultList();
```

We can see three things from this example:

- The created query is type safe and results can be obtained without casting
- The code is not as readable as the corresponding code that uses SQL or JPQL
- Since we are dealing with a Java API, the Java compiler ensures that it is not possible to create syntactically incorrect queries

The Criteria API is a great tool if we have to create dynamic queries. The creation of dynamic queries is easier because we can deal with objects instead of building query strings manually. Unfortunately, when the complexity of the created query grows, the creation of the query definition object can be troublesome and the code becomes harder to understand.

Redis

Redis is an in-memory data store that keeps its entire data set in a memory and uses disk space only as a secondary persistent storage. Therefore, Redis can provide very fast read and write operations. The catch is that the size of the Redis data set cannot be higher than the amount of memory. The other features of Redis include:

- Support for complex data types
- Multiple persistence mechanisms
- Master-slave replication
- Implementation of the publish/subscribe messaging pattern

These features are described in the following subsections.

Supported data types

Each value stored by Redis has a key. Both keys and values are binary safe, which means that the key or the stored value can be either a string or the content of a binary file. However, Redis is more than just a simple key-value store. It supports multiple binary safe data types, which should be familiar to every programmer. These data types are as follows:

- **String**: This is a data type where one key always refers to a single value.
- **List**: This is a data type where one key refers to multiple string values, which are sorted in insertion order.
- **Set**: This is a collection of unordered strings that cannot contain the same value more than once.
- **Sorted set**: This is similar to a set but each of its values has a score which is used to order the values of a sorted set from the lowest score to the highest. The same score can be assigned to multiple values.
- **Hash**: This is a data type where a single hash key always refers to a specific map of string keys and values.

Persistence

Redis supports two persistence mechanisms that can be used to store the data set on disk. They are as follows:

- **RDB** is the simplest persistence mechanism of Redis. It takes snapshots from the in-memory data sets at configured intervals, and stores the snapshot on disk. When a server is started, it will read the data set back to the memory from the snapshot file. This is the default persistence mechanism of Redis.

  RDB maximizes the performance of your Redis server, and its file format is really compact, which makes it a very useful tool for disaster recovery. Also, if you want to use the master-slave replication, you have to use RDB because the RDB snapshots are used when the data is synchronized between the master and the slaves.

  However, if you have to minimize the chance of data loss in all situations, RDB is not the right solution for you. Because RDB persists the data at configured intervals, you can always lose the data stored in to your Redis instance after the last snapshot was saved to a disk.

- **Append Only File (AOF)** is a persistence model, which logs each operation changing the state of the in-memory data set to a specific log file. When a Redis instance is started, it will reconstruct the data set by executing all operations found from the log file.

  The advantage of the AOF is that it minimizes that chance of data loss in all situations. Also, since the log file is an append log, it cannot be irreversibly corrupted. On the other hand, AOF log files are usually larger than RDB files for the same data, and AOF can be slower than RDB if the server is experiencing a huge write load.

You can also enable both persistence mechanisms and get the best of both worlds. You can use RDB for creating backups of your data set and still ensure that your data is safe. In this case, Redis will use the AOF log file for building the data set on a server startup because it is most likely that it contains the latest data.

If you are using Redis as a temporary data storage and do not need persistency, you can disable both persistence mechanisms. This means that the data sets will be destroyed when the server is shut down.

Replication

Redis supports master-slave replication where a single master can have one or multiple slaves. Each slave is an exact copy of its master, and it can connect to both master and other slaves. In other words, a slave can be a master of other slaves. Since Redis 2.6, each slave is read-only by default, and all write operations to a slave are rejected. If we need to store temporary information to a slave, we have to configure that slave to allow write operations.

Replication is non-blocking on both sides. It will not block the queries made to the master even when a slave or slaves are synchronizing their data for the very first time. Slaves can be configured to serve the old data when they are synchronizing their data with the master. However, incoming connections to a slave will be blocked for a short period of time when the old data is replaced with the new data.

If a slave loses connection to the master, it will either continue serving the old data or return an error to the clients, depending on its configuration. When a connection between master and a slave is lost, the slave will automatically reopen the connection and send a synchronization request to the master.

Publish/subscribe messaging pattern

The publish/subscribe messaging pattern is a messaging pattern where the message sender (publisher) does not send messages directly to the receiver (subscriber). Instead, an additional element called a **channel** is used to transport messages from the publisher to the subscriber. Publishers can send a message to one or more channels. Subscribers can select the interesting channels and receive messages sent to these channels by subscribing to those channels.

Let's think of a situation where a single publisher is publishing messages to two channels, Channel 1 and Channel 2. Channel 1 has two subscribers: Subscriber 1 and Subscriber 2. Channel 2 also has two subscribers: Subscriber 2 and Subscriber 3. This situation is illustrated in the following figure:

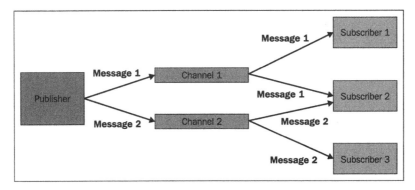

The publish/subscribe pattern ensures that the publishers are not aware of the subscribers and vice versa. This gives us the possibility to divide our application into smaller modules, which have loose coupling between them. This makes the modules easier to maintain and replace if needed.

However, the greatest advantage of the publish/subscribe pattern is also its greatest weakness. Firstly, our application cannot rely on the fact that a specific component has subscribed to a specific channel. Secondly, there is no clean way for us to verify if this is the case. In fact, our application cannot assume that anyone is listening.

Redis offers a solid support for the publish/subscribe pattern. The main features of its publish/subscribe implementation are:

- Publishers can publish messages to one or more channels at the same time
- Subscribers can subscribe to the interesting channels by using the name of the channel or a pattern containing a wildcard
- Unsubscribing from channels also supports both name and pattern matching

Summary

In this chapter, we have learned that:

- Java Persistence API was introduced to address the concerns related to EJB 2.x and to provide a standard approach for object-relational mapping. Its features were selected from the features of the most popular third party persistence frameworks.
- Redis is an in-memory data store, which keeps its entire data set in memory, supports complex data types, can use disk as a persistent storage, and supports master-slave replication. It also has an implementation of the publish/subscribe messaging pattern.

In the next chapter we will learn how we can set up a web application project that uses Spring Data JPA and use it to implement a simple contact manager application.

2
Getting Started with Spring Data JPA

This chapter gives us the basic knowledge that we need to set up a web application project and manage our entities by using Spring Data JPA. In the course of this chapter, we will learn:

- How to use **Maven** for downloading the required dependencies
- How to use **programmatic configuration** for configuring the Spring **application context**
- How to configure our web application to load the Spring application context by using programmatic configuration (without using web.xml)
- How to implement **CRUD** (**Create**, **Read**, **Update,** and **Delete**) functions for an entity class with Spring Data JPA

Downloading dependencies with Maven

This book covers the 1.2.0.RELEASE version of Spring Data JPA, which is the newest available version during the authoring of this book. The other components required by Spring Data JPA are described in the following table:

Component	Description	Version
Data source	BoneCP is a fast connection pool library that is used as a data source for our application.	0.7.1.RELEASE
JPA provider	A JPA provider is a library that implements the Java Persistence API. We will use Hibernate as a JPA provider.	4.1.4.Final

Component	Description	Version
Spring Framework	Spring Framework is used to develop modern enterprise applications with Java.	3.1.2.RELEASE
Database	H2 is an embedded in-memory database that supports standard SQL and the JDBC API.	1.3.166

We will use the newest available version of our application's other dependencies.

We can download the required dependencies with Maven by declaring them in the POM file. In order to do this, we have to add the following dependency declarations to the dependencies section of the pom.xml file:

```
<!-- Spring Data JPA -->
<dependency>
  <groupId>org.springframework.data</groupId>
  <artifactId>spring-data-jpa</artifactId>
  <version>1.2.0.RELEASE</version>
</dependency>
<!-- Hibernate -->
<dependency>
  <groupId>org.hibernate</groupId>
  <artifactId>hibernate-core</artifactId>
  <version>4.1.4.Final</version>
</dependency>
<dependency>
  <groupId>org.hibernate</groupId>
  <artifactId>hibernate-entitymanager</artifactId>
  <version>4.1.4.Final</version>
</dependency>
<!-- H2 Database -->
<dependency>
  <groupId>com.h2database</groupId>
  <artifactId>h2</artifactId>
  <version>1.3.166</version>
</dependency>
<!-- BoneCP -->
<dependency>
  <groupId>com.jolbox</groupId>
  <artifactId>bonecp</artifactId>
  <version>0.7.1.RELEASE</version>
</dependency>
```

Downloading the example code

You can download the example code files for all Packt books you have purchased from your account at http://www.packtpub.com. If you purchased this book elsewhere, you can visit http://www.packtpub.com/support and register to have the files e-mailed directly to you.

Configuring the Spring application context

Traditionally, we would use declarative configuration with XML configuration files, but after Spring Framework 3.0 was released, it has been possible to configure the Spring application context by using programmatic configuration. This is our weapon of choice when we are configuring the application context of our application.

We can configure the Spring application context by following these steps:

1. Create a properties file for the values of the configuration parameters.
2. Create the application context configuration class.

Creating the properties file

The actual values of the configuration parameters are stored in a properties file called application.properties. This file contains database connection details, Hibernate configuration, and the base package of our entities. The content of this file is as follows:

```
#Database Configuration
db.driver=org.h2.Driver
db.url=jdbc:h2:mem:datajpa
db.username=sa
db.password=

#Hibernate Configuration
hibernate.dialect=org.hibernate.dialect.H2Dialect
hibernate.format_sql=true
hibernate.hbm2ddl.auto=create-drop
hibernate.ejb.naming_strategy=org.hibernate.cfg.ImprovedNamingStrategy
hibernate.show_sql=true

#EntityManager
entitymanager.packages.to.scan=com.packtpub.springdata.jpa.model

#General Spring configuration is added here.
```

Creating the application context configuration class

We can create the application context configuration class by following these steps:

1. Create an application context configuration skeleton that contains the general configuration of the application.
2. Configure the data source bean.
3. Configure the entity manager factory bean.
4. Configure the transaction manager bean.

Creating the application context configuration skeleton

The steps that are needed to create a skeleton configuration class of the Spring application context are described in the following steps:

1. The `@Configuration` annotation identifies the class as an application context configuration class.
2. The component scanning directives are configured with the `@ComponentScan` annotation. In our example, the Spring IoC container is configured to scan the packages containing our controller and service classes.
3. The `@EnableJpaRepositories` annotation is used to enable Spring Data JPA and configure the base package of our repositories.
4. The `@EnableTransactionManagement` annotation enables the annotation-driven transaction management of Spring Framework.
5. The `@EnableWebMcv` annotation imports the default configuration of Spring MVC.
6. The properties file containing the values of the configuration parameters is imported by using the `@PropertySource` annotation. We can access the property values stored in this file by using the implementation of the `Environment` interface that is injected by the Spring IoC container.

The source code of our application context configuration skeleton is given as follows:

```
@Configuration
@ComponentScan(basePackages = {
        "com.packtpub.springdata.jpa.controller",
        "com.packtpub.springdata.jpa.service"
})
```

```
@EnableJpaRepositories("com.packtpub.springdata.jpa.repository")
@EnableTransactionManagement
@EnableWebMvc
@PropertySource("classpath:application.properties")
public class ApplicationContext extends WebMvcConfigurerAdapter {

    @Resource
    private Environment env;

    //Add configuration here
}
```

 We can also configure Spring Data JPA by using XML. We can do this by adding the repositories namespace element of Spring Data JPA to our application context configuration file.

Configuring the data source bean

We will start the configuration of the data source bean by adding a dataSource() method to the ApplicationContext class and annotating this method with the @Bean annotation. The implementation of this method is as follows:

1. Create an instance of the BoneCPDataSource class.

2. Set the database connection details.

3. Return the created object.

The configuration of the data source bean is given as follows:

```
@Bean
public DataSource dataSource() {
  BoneCPDataSource ds = new BoneCPDataSource();

  ds.setDriverClass(env.getRequiredProperty("db.driver"));
  ds.setJdbcUrl(env.getRequiredProperty("db.url"));
  ds.setUsername(env.getRequiredProperty("db.username"));
  ds.setPassword(env.getRequiredProperty("db.password"));

  return ds;
}
```

Configuring the entity manager factory bean

We can configure the entity manager factory bean by adding a method called entityManagerFactory() to the ApplicationContext class and annotating that method with the @Bean annotation. The implementation of this method is as follows:

1. Create an instance of the LocalContainerEntityManagerFactoryBean class.

2. Pass a reference of the used data source bean to the created object.

3. Set the default configuration of Hibernate to the entity manager factory bean. We can do this by creating a new HibernateJpaVendorAdapter object and passing it to the entity manager factory bean.

4. Set the base package of our entities.

5. Set the additional configuration that is fetched from our properties file.

6. Return the created object.

The source code of the created method is given as follows:

```
@Bean
public LocalContainerEntityManagerFactoryBean entityManagerFactory() {
    LocalContainerEntityManagerFactoryBean em = new
LocalContainerEntityManagerFactoryBean();

    em.setDataSource(dataSource());
    em.setJpaVendorAdapter(new HibernateJpaVendorAdapter());
em.setPackagesToScan(env.getRequiredProperty("entitymanager.packages.
to.scan"));

    Properties p = new Properties();
    p.put("hibernate.dialect", env.getRequiredProperty("hibernate.
dialect"));
    p.put("hibernate.format_sql", env.getRequiredProperty("hibernate.
format_sql"));
    p.put("hibernate.hbm2ddl.auto", env.
getRequiredProperty("hibernate.hbm2ddl.auto"));
    p.put("hibernate.ejb.naming_strategy", env.
getRequiredProperty("hibernate.ejb.naming_strategy"));
    p.put("hibernate.show_sql", env.getRequiredProperty("hibernate.
show_sql"));
    em.setJpaProperties(p);

    return em;
}
```

Configuring the transaction manager bean

We can configure the transaction manager bean by adding a `transactionManager()` method to the `ApplicationContext` class and annotating this method with the `@Bean` annotation. The implementation of this method is as follows:

1. Create a new `JpaTransactionManager` object.
2. Set a reference of the used entity manager factory.
3. Return the created object.

The source code of the transaction manager bean configuration is given as follows:

```
@Bean
public JpaTransactionManager transactionManager() {
    JpaTransactionManager transactionManager = new
JpaTransactionManager();
    transactionManager.setEntityManagerFactory(entityManagerFactory().
getObject());
    return transactionManager;
}
```

Loading the application context configuration

The old way to load the application context configuration of our application is to use the **web application deployment descriptor** file, which is more commonly known as `web.xml`. However, because we are using the Spring Framework 3.1 in a Servlet 3.0 environment, we can create a web application configuration class by implementing the `WebApplicationInitializer` interface. This ensures that Spring Framework automatically detects our configuration class when a servlet container is started.

We will use our web application configuration class to:

1. Load our application context configuration class.
2. Configure the **dispatcher servlet**.
3. Create the **context loader listener** and add it to our **servlet context**.

The source code of our configuration class is given as follows:

```
public class DataJPAExampleInitializer implements
WebApplicationInitializer {

    @Override
    public void onStartup(ServletContext servletContext) throws
ServletException {
```

```
        //Loading application context
        AnnotationConfigWebApplicationContext rootContext = new
AnnotationConfigWebApplicationContext();
        rootContext.register(ApplicationContext.class);

        //Dispatcher servlet
        ServletRegistration.Dynamic dispatcher = servletContext.
addServlet("dispatcher", new DispatcherServlet(rootContext));
        dispatcher.setLoadOnStartup(1);
        dispatcher.addMapping("/");

        //Context loader listener
        servletContext.addListener(new ContextLoaderListener(rootCont
ext));
    }
}
```

Implementing CRUD functionality for an entity

We have now configured the Spring application context and configured our web application to load it during startup. We will now implement CRUD functions for a simple entity. Our example application is used to view and manage contact information, and we can implement it by following these steps:

1. Create a domain model.
2. Create a repository for an entity.
3. Implement CRUD functions.

 This chapter describes only such parts of our application that are required to understand how Spring Data JPA works.

Domain model

The domain model of our application consists of two classes: Contact and Address. This subsection will address the following matters:

* The information content of each class
* How we can create new objects by using the **builder pattern** (see also: *Effective Java* (*Second Edition*), *Joshua Bloch, Addison-Wesley*)
* How we can update the information of an object

Contact

The Contact class is the only entity of our domain model and it contains the information of a single contact. This information consists mostly of simple properties. The only exception to this rule is the Address class that is used to store address information. The relevant parts of the Contact class' source code is given as follows:

```
@Entity
@Table(name = "contacts")
public class Contact {

    @Id
    @GeneratedValue(strategy = GenerationType.AUTO)
    private Long id;

    private Address address;

    @Column(name = "email_address", length = 100)
    private String emailAddress;

    @Column(name = "first_name", nullable=false, length = 50)
    private String firstName;

    @Column(name = "last_name", nullable=false, length = 100)
    private String lastName;

    @Column(name = "phone_number", length = 30)
    private String phoneNumber;

    @Version
    private long version;

    //Getters and other methods
}
```

Let's move on and find out how we can create new contacts and update contact information.

Creating new contact objects

We will use the builder pattern for creating new contacts. In order to do so, we have to follow these steps:

1. Implement a static inner class that is used to build new Contact objects.
2. Add a static getBuilder() method to the Contact class. This method is used to get a reference to the used builder.

We will start by adding a static inner class to the Contact class by following these steps:

1. Implement a constructor that takes the required properties as parameters. The required properties of a contact are first name and last name.
2. Implement property methods for optional properties. These properties include e-mail address, phone number, and address information. Each property method returns a reference to the used builder object.
3. Implement a build() method that returns the build object.

The source code of the Contact.Builder class is given as follows:

```
public static class Builder {

        private Contact built;

        public Builder (String firstName, String lastName) {
            built = new Contact();
            built.firstName = firstName;
            built.lastName = lastName;
        }

        public Builder address(String streetAddress, String postCode,
    String postOffice, String state, String country) {
            Address address = Address.getBuilder(streetAddress,
    postCode, postOffice)
                    .state(state)
                    .country(country)
                    .build();
            built.address = address;
            return this;
        }

        public Builder emailAddress(String emailAddress) {
            built.emailAddress = emailAddress;
            return this;
```

```
        }

        public Builder phoneNumber(String phoneNumber) {
            built.phoneNumber = phoneNumber;
            return this;
        }

        public Contact build() {
            return built;
        }
    }
}
```

We have to also add a static getBuilder() method to the Contact class. Our implementation is pretty straightforward. We create a new Contact.Builder object and return the created object. The source code of this method is given as follows:

```
public static Builder getBuilder(String firstName, String lastName) {
    return new Builder(firstName, lastName);
}
```

Updating contact information

The Contact class has two methods that we can use to update contact information: the update() method that updates the contact information and the updateAddress() method that updates the address information of the contact. The source code of these methods is given as follows:

```
public void update(final String firstName, final String lastName,
final String emailAddress, final String phoneNumber) {
    this.firstName = firstName;
    this.lastName = lastName;
    this.emailAddress = emailAddress;
    this.phoneNumber = phoneNumber;
}

public void updateAddress(final String streetAddress, final String
postCode, final String postOffice, final String state, final String
country) {
    if (address == null) {
        address = new Address();
    }
    address.update(streetAddress, postCode, postOffice, state,
country);
}
```

Address

The Address class is an embedded class that is used to store address information. An **embedded class** is a class that can be persisted only with its parent class. Embedded classes are typically used to present the common concepts of the domain model and to emphasize its object-oriented nature. The source code of the Address class is given as follows:

```
@Embeddable
public class Address {

    @Column(name = "country", length = 20)
    private String country;

    @Column(name = "street_address", length =150)
    private String streetAddress;

    @Column(name = "post_code", length = 10)
    private String postCode;

    @Column(name = "post_office", length = 40)
    private String postOffice;

    @Column(name = "state", length = 20)
    private String state;

    //The default constructor and other methods
}
```

Next, we will find out how we can create new Address objects and update the address information of existing objects.

Creating new addresses

We will create new Address objects by using the builder pattern. We can implement the builder pattern by following these steps:

1. Implement a static inner class that is used to build new Address objects.

2. Add a static getBuilder() method to the Address class. This method is used to get a reference to the used builder.

We can implement the static inner class by following these steps:

1. Implement a constructor that takes the required properties as parameters. The required properties of the Address class are streetAddress, postCode, and postOffice.

2. Implement property methods that are used to set optional address information. This information includes state and country. Each property method returns a reference to the used builder.

3. Implement a `build()` method that returns the build object.

The source code of the `Address.Builder` class is given as follows:

```
public static class Builder {

  private Address built;

  public Builder(String streetAddress, String postCode, String
postOffice) {
    built = new Address();
    built.streetAddress = streetAddress;
    built.postCode = postCode;
    built.postOffice = postOffice;
  }

  public Builder country(String country) {
    built.country = country;
    return this;
  }

  public Builder state(String state) {
    built.state = state;
    return this;
  }

  public Address build() {
    return built;
    }
}
```

We must also implement a method that is used to get a reference to the used builder object. We can do this by simply creating a new `Address.Builder` object and returning the created object. The source code of the static `getBuilder()` method of the `Address` class is given as follows:

```
public static Builder getBuilder(String streetAddress, String
postCode, String postOffice) {
    return new Builder(streetAddress, postCode, postOffice);
}
```

Updating address information

We can update the information of an `Address` object by calling its `update()` method. The source code of this method is given as follows:

```
public void update(final String streetAddress, final String postCode,
final String postOffice, final String state, final String country) {
    this.streetAddress = streetAddress;
    this.postCode = postCode;
    this.postOffice = postOffice;
    this.state = state;
    this.country = country;
}
```

Creating a custom repository

In order to truly understand the simplicity of Spring Data JPA, we must take a trip to a not so distant past and learn how concrete repositories were created before Spring Data JPA was released. This should give us a clear picture about the benefits of Spring Data JPA.

Creating a custom repository in the old school way

Traditionally, the creation of concrete repositories has been a process that includes six steps. They are as follows:

1. Create a base class that provides property mappings for its subclasses. It is often used to provide ID, version, and timestamp mappings for our entities.
2. Create a generic repository interface that declares the methods shared by all repositories. Typically these methods provide CRUD operations for our entities.
3. Create a generic repository.
4. Create an entity class.
5. Create an entity specific repository interface.
6. Create an entity specific concrete repository.

First, we have to create an abstract base class that is extended by each entity class. We can create this class by following these steps:

1. Create an abstract class that takes the type of the entity's ID as a type parameter.
2. Annotate the created class with `@MappedSuperclass` annotation. It is used to state that the mappings found from this class are applied to its subclasses.
3. Create an abstract `getId()` method that returns the ID of a concrete class.

The source code of the `BaseEntity` class is given as follows:

```
@MappedSuperclass
public abstract class BaseEntity<ID> {

    @Version
    private Long version;

    public abstract ID getId();
}
```

Second, we have to create a generic repository interface that declares the methods shared by all concrete repositories. We can create this interface by following these steps:

1. Add the type of the entity and the type of the entity's ID as type parameters.
2. Declare the methods that are shared by all concrete repositories.

The source code of the `BaseRepository` interface is as follows:

```
public interface BaseRepository<T extends BaseEntity, ID extends
Serializable> {

    public T deleteById(ID id);
    public List<T> findAll();
    public T findById(ID id);
    public void persist(T entity);
}
```

Third, we must create an abstract generic repository. We can do this by following these steps:

1. Create an abstract class that takes the type of the concrete entity and the type of the entity's ID as a type parameter.
2. Get a reference to the used entity manager by using the `@PersistenceContext` annotation.
3. Implement the `BaseRepository` interface.
4. Implement a constructor that fetches the type of the entity class from the type parameters.

5. Provide a `getEntityManager()` method that returns a reference to the used entity manager. The subclasses of this class will use this method for obtaining the entity manager reference that is used to build database queries.

6. Provide a `getEntityClass()` method that returns the type of the entity. Subclasses use this method to build database queries by using the Criteria API.

The source code of the `BaseRepositoryImpl` class is given as follows:

```
public abstract class BaseRepositoryImpl<T extends BaseEntity, ID
extends Serializable> implements BaseRepository<T, ID> {

    private Class<T> entityClass;

    @PersistenceContext(unitName = "pu")
    private EntityManager em;

    public BaseDAOImpl() {
        this.entityClass = ((Class<T>) ((ParameterizedType)
getClass().getGenericSuperclass()).getActualTypeArguments()[0]);
    }

    @Override
    @Transactional(propagation = Propagation.REQUIRED)
    public T deleteById(ID id) {
        T entity = findById(id);
        if (entity != null) {
            em.remove(entity);
        }
        return entity;
    }

    @Override
    public List<T> findAll() {
        CriteriaBuilder cb = em.getCriteriaBuilder();
        CriteriaQuery<T> query = cb.createQuery(entityClass);
        Root<T> root = query.from(entityClass);
        return em.createQuery(query).getResultList();
    }

    @Override
    public T findById(ID id) {
        return em.find(getEntityClass(), id);
```

```
    }

    @Override
    @Transactional(propagation = Propagation.REQUIRED)
    public void persist(T entity) {
        em.persist(entity);
    }

    protected Class<T> getEntityClass() {
        return entityClass;
    }

    protected EntityManager getEntityManager() {
        return em;
    }
}
```

Next, we must create an entity class. We can create this class by following these steps:

1. Extend the `BaseEntity` class and provide the type of the entity's ID as a type parameter.

2. Implement the `getId()` method that returns the entity's ID.

The source code of the `Contact` class is given as follows:

```
@Entity
@Table(name = "contacts")
public class Contact extends BaseEntity<Long> {

    @Id
    @GeneratedValue(strategy = GenerationType.AUTO) private Long id;

    @Override
    public Long getId() {
        return id;
    }
}
```

Next, we must create an interface for our entity specific repository. We can do this by extending the `BaseRepository` interface and providing the type of our entity and the type of its ID as type parameters. The source code of the `ContactRepository` interface is given as follows:

```
public interface ContactRepository extends BaseRepository<Contact,
Long> {
    //Declare custom methods here.
}
```

Next, we must create the entity specific concrete repository. We can create a concrete repository by following these steps:

1. Annotate the concrete repository class with `@Repository` annotation that identifies the created class as a repository class.

2. Extend the `BaseRepositoryImpl` class and give the type of the entity and the type of the entity's ID as a type parameter.

3. Implement the `ContactRepository` interface.

The source code of the `ContactRepositoryImpl` class is as follows:

```
@Repository
public class ContactRepositoryImpl extends BaseRepositoryImpl<Contact,
Long> implements ContactRepository {
    //Add custom query methods here
}
```

Congratulations! We have now created a single concrete repository in the old fashioned way. The structure of our repository implementation is illustrated in the following figure:

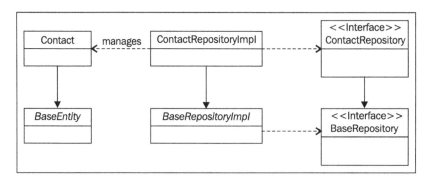

As we have noticed, implementing concrete repositories is a complicated process that takes a lot of time, which we could spend being actually productive. Luckily, this is not the only way to create repositories for our entities. Next we will learn a simpler and easier way to create custom repositories. Naturally, we are talking about Spring Data JPA.

Creating a custom repository with Spring Data JPA

Spring Data JPA is capable of creating concrete repository implementations automatically from special repository interfaces. This capability simplifies the creation process of custom repositories.

We can create a JPA repository for an entity by creating an interface, which extends the JpaRepository interface. When we are extending the JpaRepository interface, we have to provide two type parameters: the type of the entity and the type of the entity's object identifier.

In our case, we need to create a repository for the Contact entity. The type of its object identifier is Long. Thus, the source code of the ContactRepository interface should look like the following:

```
public interface ContactRepository extends JpaRepository<Contact,
Long> {
}
```

That is all. We have now created a repository for the Contact entity. The structure of our repository implementation is illustrated in the following figure:

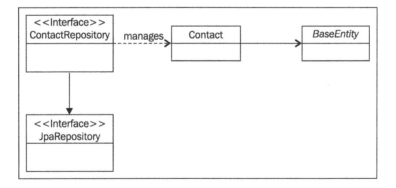

As we can see, the creation of a custom repository could not be any simpler than this. Spring Data JPA reduces the amount of code we need to write and maintain, and the time that is needed to write it. In other words, we can get the same functionality by writing simpler code in a shorter time. This perk is pretty hard to beat.

extending the `JpaRepository` interface, we have now gained access to four thods that are needed for implementing the CRUD application. These methods are described in the following table:

Method	Description
`Void delete(Contact contact)`	Deletes a single contact from the database.
`Contact findOne(Long id)`	Returns a single contact or null if no contact is found.
`List<Contact> findAll()`	Returns all contacts stored to the database.
`Contact save(Contact contact)`	Saves the given contact to the database and returns the saved contact.

CRUD

We have now configured the Spring application context, implemented the domain model of our application, and created the repository for the `Contact` entity. We are finally ready to write the source code of the service class that provides CRUD functions for the `Contact` entity.

Let's start by creating an interface for our service. Its role is to declare the methods used to handle contact information. Let's call this interface `ContactService`. The source code of our interface is given as follows:

```
public interface ContactService {

    public Contact add(ContactDTO added);
    public Contact deleteById(Long id) throws NotFoundException;
    public List<Contact> findAll();
    public Contact findById(Long id) throws NotFoundException;
    public Contact update(ContactDTO updated) throws
NotFoundException;
}
```

The `ContactService` interface mentions a class called `ContactDTO`. It is a **data transfer object (DTO)** used to pass information to our service implementation. This DTO is used as a form object in the web layer of our application and it contains only the information needed to add or update contact information. In other words, it has no logic in it. That is why its source code is not discussed here.

The concept of data transfer objects is described at `http://martinfowler.com/eaaCatalog/dataTransferObject.html`.

Our next step is to create an implementation to the `ContactService` interface. Let's start by creating a dummy implementation and add the actual logic later. The dummy service implementation is described as follows:

1. The `@Service` annotation is used to mark our implementation as a service class. By adding this annotation we ensure that the class will be automatically detected during classpath scanning.

2. We use the `@Resource` annotation to tell the Spring **IoC container** that it has to inject the created repository implementation to the service's `repository` field.

 Each method of the service class is marked as transactional by using the `@Transactional` annotation. The `rollbackFor` configuration option ensures that the transaction is rolled back if any of the configured exceptions is thrown.

The source code of our dummy service class is given as follows:

```
@Service
public class RepositoryContactService implements ContactService {

    @Resource
    private ContactRepository repository;

    //Empty method skeletons
}
```

Next we will get our hands dirty and learn how we can create, read, update, and delete entities with Spring Data JPA.

Create

We can create a new entity by following these steps:

1. Create a new `Contact` object by using the builder pattern.
2. Pass the created object to the `save()` method of our repository.
3. Return the created object.

The source code of the `add()` method is given as follows:

```
@Transactional
@Override
public Contact add(ContactDTO added) {
    //Creates an instance of a Contact by using the builder pattern
```

```
        Contact contact = Contact.getBuilder(added.getFirstName(), added.
getLastName())
                .address(added.getStreetAddress(), added.getPostCode(),
added.getPostOffice(), added.getState(), added.getCountry())
                .emailAddress(added.getEmailAddress())
                .phoneNumber(added.getPhoneNumber())
                .build();
        return repository.save(contact);
    }
```

Read

Our application has to provide a list of all contacts and the information of a single contact to its user. The ContactService interface declares two methods, which are relevant to these use cases. These methods are: findAll() and findById().

Our implementation of the findAll() method is fairly simple. We simply delegate the method call forward to the repository. The source code of the findAll() method is given as follows:

```
@Transactional(readOnly = true)
@Override
public List<Contact> findAll() {
    return repository.findAll();
}
```

Now we have to create an implementation of the findById() method. Our implementation contains the following steps:

1. Find the contact by calling our repository's findOne() method.
2. If no contact is found, throw a NotFoundException.
3. Return the found contact.

The source code of the findById() method is given as follows:

```
@Transactional(readOnly = true)
@Override
public Contact findById(Long id) throws NotFoundException {
    Contact found = repository.findOne(id);

    if (found == null) {
        throw new NotFoundException("No contact found with id: " +
id);
```

```
    }

    return found;
}
```

Update

We can update the information of a contact by following these steps:

1. Use the service's `findById()` method for finding the updated contact. Thus, if no contact is found, a `NotFoundException` is thrown.

2. Update the contact information.

3. Update the address information.

4. Return the updated contact.

The source code of the `update()` method is given as follows:

```
@Transactional(rollbackFor = NotFoundException.class)
@Override
public Contact update(ContactDTO updated) throws NotFoundException {
    Contact found = findById(updated.getId());

    found.update(updated.getFirstName(), updated.getLastName(),
updated.getEmailAddress(), updated.getPhoneNumber());

    found.updateAddress(updated.getStreetAddress(), updated.
getPostCode(), updated.getPostOffice(), updated.getState(), updated.
getCountry());

    return found;
}
```

We don't have to explicitly call the `save()` method of a repository after we update the information of an entity if we are inside a read-write transaction. All changes made to a persistent entity are automatically updated to the database when the transaction is committed.

Delete

We can delete a contact by following these steps:

1. Find the deleted contact by calling the `findById()` method that throws a `NotFoundException` if no contact is found.

2. Pass the contact to our repository's `delete()` as a parameter.

3. Return the deleted contact.

The source code of the `deleteById()` method is given as follows:

```
@Transactional(rollbackFor = NotFoundException.class)
@Override
public Contact deleteById(Long id) throws NotFoundException {
    Contact deleted = findById(id);
    repository.delete(deleted);
    return deleted;
}
```

Summary

In this chapter, we have learned that:

- Maven provides an easy way to set up a Spring Data JPA project
- We can configure the application context of our application by using programmatic configuration if we use Spring Framework 3.0 or newer versions
- If we use Spring Framework 3.1 in a Servlet 3.0 environment, we can configure our web application without `web.xml`
- Spring Data JPA simplifies the creation of custom repositories because it can automatically create concrete implementations of our repository interfaces

Building a CRUD application is a good start but it does not help us create real-life applications. In the next chapter, we will address this issue and describe how we can create database queries with Spring Data JPA.

3
Building Queries with Spring Data JPA

We have learned how we can configure Spring Data JPA and implemented a simple CRUD application. Now it is time that we learn some skills that will help us to implement real-life applications. In this chapter, we will cover:

- How we can use query methods for creating queries
- How we can create dynamic queries by using the JPA Criteria API
- How we can use Querydsl for creating dynamic queries
- How we can sort and paginate query results

In the course of this chapter, we will extend our contact manager application by adding a search function to it. The requirements of the search function are as follows:

- The search function must return all contacts whose first name or last name start with the given search term
- The search must be case insensitive
- The search results must be sorted in ascending order by using the last name and first name
- The search function must be able to paginate search results

We will also learn to sort and paginate the contact list shown on the home page of our application.

Building queries

There are three options we can use to build queries with Spring Data JPA: query methods, JPA Criteria API, and Querydsl. During this section, we will learn how to use them and start the implementation of our search function. We will also take a look at the pros and cons of each option and receive concrete recommendations concerning the selection of the correct query creation technique.

Before we can move forward, we have to add a `search()` method, which is used as a starting point of our search function, to the `ContactService` interface. The signature of the `search()` method looks like the following code snippet:

```
public List<Contact> search(String searchTerm);
```

Query methods

The simplest way to create queries with Spring Data JPA is to use query methods. **Query methods** are methods that are declared in the repository interface. There are three techniques we can use to create query methods:

- **Query generation from method name**
- **Named Queries**
- The `@Query` annotation

Query generation from method name

Query generation from method name is a query generation strategy where the executed query is parsed from the name of a query method. The naming convention, which is used to create the names of query methods, has three important components: **method prefixes**, **property expressions**, and **keywords**. Next we will learn the basic usage of these components and implement our search function. We will also take a look at the pros and cons of this approach.

Method prefixes

The name of each method must start with a special prefix. This ensures that the method is identified as a query method. The supported prefixes are `findBy`, `find`, `readBy`, `read`, `getBy`, and `get`. All prefixes are synonyms and they have no effect on the parsed query.

Property expressions

Property expressions are used to refer either to a direct property or to a nested property of a managed entity. We will use the Contact entity to demonstrate the usage of property expressions in the following table:

Property expression	Referred property
LastName	The lastName property of the Contact class.
AddressStreetAddress	The streetAddress property of the Address class.

Let's find out how the property resolution algorithm works by using the AddressStreetAddress property expression as an example. This algorithm has three phases:

1. At first it will check if the entity class has a property with the name matching the property expression when the first letter of the property expression is transformed to lowercase. If a match is found, that property is used. If a property named addressStreetAddress is not found from the Contact class the algorithm moves to the next phase.

2. The property expression is split at camel case parts starting from right to left to a head and a tail. After this is done, the algorithm tries to find a matching property from the entity. If a match it found, the algorithm tries to find the referred property by following the parts of the property expression from head to tail. In this phase, our property expression is split into two parts: AddressStreet and Address. Since the Contact entity does not have a matching property, the algorithm continues to the third phase.

3. The split point is moved to the left and the algorithm tries to find a matching property from the entity. The property expression is split into two parts: Address and StreetAddress. A matching property address is found from the Contact class. Also, since the Address class has a property named streetAddress, a match is found.

> If the Contact class would have a property called addressStreetAddress, the property selection algorithm would select it instead of the streetAddress property of the Address class. We can solve this problem by using the underscore character in the property expression to manually specify traversal points. In this case, we should use a property expression Address_StreetAddress.

Keywords

Keywords are used to specify constraints against the values of properties referred by property expressions. There are two rules that are used to combine property expressions together with keywords:

- We can create a **constraint** by adding a keyword after a property expression
- We can combine constraints by adding either the **And** or **Or** keyword between them

The reference manual of Spring Data JPA (`http://static.springsource.org/spring-data/data-jpa/docs/current/reference/html/`) describes how property expressions and keywords can be used for creating query methods:

Keyword	Sample	JPQL Snippet
And	findByLastNameAndFirstName	where x.lastname = ?1 and x.firstname = ?2
Or	findByLastNameOrFirstName	where x.lastname = ?1 or x.firstname = ?2
Between	findByStartDateBetween	where x.startDate between 1? and ?2
LessThan	findByAgeLessThan	where x.age < ?1
GreaterThan	findByAgeGreaterThan	where x.age > ?1
After	findByStartDateAfter	where x.startDate > ?1
Before	findByStartDateBefore	where x.startDate < ?1
IsNull	findByAgeIsNull	where x.age is null
IsNotNull, NotNull	findByAge(Is)NotNull	where x.age is not null
Like	findByFirstNameLike	where x.firstname like ?1
NotLike	findByFirstNameNotLike	where x.firstname not like ?1
StartingWith	findByFirstNameStartingWith	where x.firstname like ?1 (parameter bound with appended %)
EndingWith	findByFirstNameEndingWith	where x.firstname like ?1 (parameter bound with prepended %)

Keyword	Sample	JPQL Snippet
Containing	findByFirstNameContaining	where x.firstname like ?1 (parameter bound wrapped in %)
OrderBy	findByAgeOrderByLastNameDesc	where x.age = ?1 order by x.lastname desc
Not	findByLastNameNot	where x.lastname <> ?1
In	findByAgeIn (Collection<Age> ages)	where x.age in ?1
NotIn	findByAgeNotIn (Collection<Age> ages)	where x.age not in ?1
True	findByActiveTrue	where x.active = true
False	findByActiveFalse	where x.active = false

Implementing the search function

It is time to use the skills we have learned and add the search function to our contact manager application. We can implement the search function by following these steps:

1. We add a query method to the ContactRepository interface by following the described naming convention.
2. We implement a service method that uses the query method.

First, we have to create the query method. The signature of our query method is given as follows:

```
public List<Contact> findByFirstNameStartingWithOrLastNameStartingWith
(String firstName, String lastName);
```

Second, we have to add the search() method to the RepositoryContactService class. This method simply delegates the method call to the repository and gives the used search term as a parameter. The source code of the implemented method is given as follows:

```
@Transactional(readOnly = true)
@Override
public List<Contact> search(String searchTerm) {
  return repository.findByFirstNameStartingWithOrLastNameStartingWith(
searchTerm, searchTerm);
}
```

Pros and cons

We have now learned how we can create queries by using the query generation from the method name strategy. The pros and cons of this strategy are described in the following table:

Pros	Cons
• It is a fast way to create simple queries • It provides a consistent naming strategy for method names	• The features of the method name parser decide what kind of queries we can create • The method names of complicated query methods are long and ugly • Queries are verified at runtime • No support for dynamic queries

One good example about the limitations of the method name parser is the lack of the Lower keyword. This means that we cannot implement a case insensitive search by using this strategy. Next we will learn alternative strategies for creating queries that do not suffer from this restriction.

Named queries

A second way to create query methods with Spring Data JPA is to use named queries. If we want to create a query method with a named query, we have to:

1. Create a named query.
2. Create a query method that executes the named query.
3. Create a service method that uses the created query method.

These steps are described with more details in following section. We will also discuss the pros and cons of named queries.

Creating a named query

Spring Data JPA supports named queries that are created by using either JPQL or SQL. The selection of the used query language determines how the created named query is declared.

We can create a JPA named query by following these steps:

1. We add the `@NamedQueries` annotation to an entity class. This annotation takes an array of `@NamedQuery` annotations as its value, and it must be used if we specify more than one named query

2. We use the `@NamedQuery` annotation for creating the named query. This annotation has two properties that are relevant to us: the `name` property stores the name of the named query, and the `query` property contains the executed JPQL query.

The declaration of our named query, which uses JPQL, is given as follows:

```
@Entity
@NamedQueries({
@NamedQuery(name = "Contact.findContacts",
        query = "SELECT c FROM Contact c WHERE LOWER(c.firstName) LIKE
LOWER(:searchTerm) OR LOWER(c.lastName) LIKE LOWER(:searchTerm)")
})
@Table(name = "contacts")
public class Contact
```

 We can also use XML for declaring named queries. In this case, we must use the `named-query` element and declare the query in an entity mapping XML file.

We can create a named native query by following these steps:

1. We add the `@NamedNativeQueries` annotation to an entity class. This annotation accepts an array of `@NamedNativeQuery` annotations as its value, and it must be used if we specify more than one native named query.

2. We create the native named query by using the `@NamedNativeQuery` annotation. The name of the created native named query is stored in the `name` property. The value of the `query` property is the executed SQL query. The `resultClass` property contains an entity class that is returned by the query.

 If the named native query does not return an entity or a list of entities, we can map the query result to a correct return type by using the `@SqlResultSetMapping` annotation.

The declaration of our named native query looks like the following code snippet:

```
@Entity
@NamedNativeQueries({
@NamedNativeQuery(name = "Contact.findContacts",
        query = "SELECT * FROM contacts c WHERE LOWER(c.
first_name) LIKE LOWER(:searchTerm) OR LOWER(c.last_name) LIKE
LOWER(:searchTerm)",
        resultClass = Contact.class)
})
@Table(name = "contacts")
public class Contact
```

 We can also use XML for creating named native queries. In this case, we must use the `named-native-query` element and declare the SQL query in an entity mapping XML file.

Creating the query method

Our next step is to add the query method to the contact repository. We will have to:

1. Determine the correct name for the query method. Spring Data JPA resolves method names back to named queries by pretending the simple name of the managed entity and a dot to the method name. The name of our named query is `Contact.findContacts`. Thus, we have to add a method called `findContacts` to the `ContactRepository` interface.

2. Use the `@Param` annotation to identify the method parameter as a value of the named parameter that is used in our queries.

The signature of the added query method is given as follows:

```
public List<Contact> findContacts(@Param("searchTerm") String
searchTerm);
```

Creating the service method

Next we have to add the `search()` method to the `RepositoryContactService` class. Our implementation consists of the following steps:

1. We build the used like pattern.
2. We fetch the search results by calling the created query method.

The source code of the `search()` method is given as follows:

```
@Transactional(readOnly = true)
@Override
public List<Contact> search(String searchTerm) {
    String likePattern = buildLikePattern(searchTerm);
    return repository.findContacts(likePattern);
}

private String buildLikePattern(String searchTerm) {
    return searchTerm + "%";
}
```

Pros and cons

We are now capable of creating query methods by using named queries. The pros and cons of this approach are described in the following table:

Pros	Cons
• Supports both JPQL and SQL	• Query validation is done at runtime
• Makes it easier to migrate existing applications using named queries to Spring Data JPA	• No support for dynamic queries
	• The query logic litters the code of our entity classes
• The return type of native queries is not restricted to entities or to the list of entities	

@Query annotation

The @Query annotation is used to specify the query that is executed when a query method is called. We can implement both JPQL and SQL queries with the @Query annotation by:

1. Adding a new method of a repository and annotating it with the @Query annotation.

2. Creating the service method, which uses the query method.

 If the method name of the method annotated with the @Query annotation conflicts with the name of a named query, the annotated query will be executed.

Next we will get concrete instructions that will guide us through the described steps and find out the pros and cons of this technique.

Creating the query method

First we must add the query method to the `ContactRepository` class. As we already know, we can create the actual query by using either JPQL or SQL. The selection of the used query language has some effects on the creation of the query methods.

We can create a query method that uses JPQL by:

1. Adding a new method to the `ContactRepository` interface.
2. Using the `@Param` annotation to identify the parameter of the method as the value of the named parameter.
3. Annotating the method with the `@Query` annotation and setting the executed JPQL query as its value.

The declaration of our query method, which fulfills the requirements of the search function, is given as follows:

```
@Query("SELECT c FROM Contact c WHERE LOWER(c.firstName) LIKE
LOWER(:searchTerm) OR LOWER(c.lastName) LIKE LOWER(:searchTerm)")
public Page<Contact> findContacts(@Param("searchTerm") String
searchTerm);
```

In order to create a query method that uses SQL, we have to:

1. Add a new method to the `ContactRepository` interface.
2. Identify the method parameter as a value of the named parameter used in the SQL query by using the `@Param` annotation.
3. Annotate the created method with the `@Query` annotation and set the SQL query as its value. Set the value of the `nativeQuery` property to true.

> A native query created with the `@Query` annotation can return only entities or list of entities. If we need a different return type, we must use a named query and map the query result by using the `@SqlResultSetMapping` annotation.

The declaration of our query method, which implements the requirements of the search function, looks like the following code snippet:

```
@Query(value = "SELECT * FROM contacts c WHERE LOWER(c.first_name)
LIKE LOWER(:searchTerm) OR LOWER(c.last_name) LIKE LOWER(:searchTerm),
nativeQuery = true)
public List<Contact> findContacts(@Param("searchTerm") String
searchTerm);
```

Spring Data JPA does not provide dynamic sorting or pagination support for native queries created with @Query annotation because there is no reliable way to manipulate SQL queries.

Creating the service method

Our next step is to add an implementation of the search() method to the RepositoryContactService class. We can do this by:

1. Getting the used like pattern.
2. Fetching the search results by calling the created query method.

The source code of the implemented search() method is given as follows:

```
@Transactional(readOnly = true)
@Override
public List<Contact> search(String searchTerm) {
    String likePattern = buildLikePattern(searchTerm);
    return repository.findContacts(likePattern);
}

private String buildLikePattern(String searchTerm) {
    return searchTerm + "%";
}
```

Pros and cons

We have now learned how we can use the @Query annotation for creating query methods. This approach naturally has both pros and cons that are described in the following table:

Pros	Cons
• Supports both JPQL and SQL • No naming convention for method names	• Native queries can return only entities or a list of entities • No support for dynamic queries • Query validation is done at runtime

JPA Criteria API

The JPA Criteria API provides us with a way to create dynamic and type-safe queries in an object-oriented manner. We can create **criteria queries** by following these steps:

1. We add JPA Criteria API support to a repository.
2. We create the executed criteria query.
3. We create a service method that executes the created query.

These steps, and the pros and cons of using the JPA criteria API, are described in the following section.

Adding the JPA Criteria API support to a repository

We can add JPA Criteria API support to a repository by extending the `JpaSpecificationExecutor<T>` interface. When we extend this interface, we must give the type of the managed entity as a type parameter. The source code of the `ContactRepository` interface is given as follows:

```
public interface ContactRepository extends JpaRepository<Contact,
Long>, JpaSpecificationExecutor<Contact> {

}
```

Extending the `JpaSpecificationExecutor<T>` interface gives us access to the following methods that can be used to execute criteria queries:

Method	Description
`long count(Specification<Contact> s)`	Returns the number of entities matching with the given search criteria.
`List<Contact> findAll(Specification<Contact> s)`	Returns all entities matching with the given search criteria.
`Contact findOne(Specification<Contact> s)`	Returns a single contact matching with the given search criteria.

Creating the criteria query

As we have learned, Spring Data JPA uses the `Specification<T>` interface for specifying the criteria query. This interface declares the `Predicate toPredicate(Root<T> root, CriteriaQuery<?> query, CriteriaBuilder cb)` method that we can use to create the executed criteria query.

In order to create criteria queries for the Contact entity, we have to:

1. Create a static metamodel class for the Contact entity.
2. Create a way to build Specification<Contact> objects.

Creating a static metamodel class

Static metamodel classes provide static access to the metadata that describes the attributes of entities, and they are used to create type-safe queries with JPA Criteria API. Static metamodel classes are typically generated automatically but in here we will create one manually for the sake of an example. We can create a static metamodel class by following these rules:

* A static metamodel class should be placed in the same package than the corresponding entity

* The name of a static metamodel class is created by appending an underscore character to the simple name of the corresponding entity

Since we are using only the firstName and lastName properties of the Contact entity when building our criteria query, we can ignore the other attributes. The source code of the Contact_ class looks like the following code:

```
@StaticMetamodel(Contact.class)
public class Contact_ {
    public static volatile SingularAttribute<Contact, String>
firstName;
    public static volatile SingularAttribute<Contact, String>
lastName;
}
```

Creating specifications

We can create specifications in a clean manner by creating a specification builder class and use static method to build the actual specifications. The logic used to build the needed like pattern is also moved to this class. Our implementation of the specification builder class is explained in the following steps:

1. We create a getLikePattern() method that is used to create the like pattern from the search term.
2. We create a static firstOrLastNameStartsWith() method that returns a new Specification<Contact> object.
3. We build the criteria query in the toPredicate() method of the Specification<Contact>.

The source code of our specification builder class is given as follows:

```java
public class ContactSpecifications {

    public static Specification<Contact>
firstOrLastNameStartsWith(final String searchTerm) {
        return new Specification<Contact>() {
        //Creates the search criteria
        @Override
        public Predicate toPredicate(Root<Contact> root,
CriteriaQuery<?> criteriaQuery, cb cb) {
            String likePattern = getLikePattern(searchTerm);
            return cb.or(
            //First name starts with given search term
            cb.like(cb.lower(root.<String>get(Contact_.firstName)),
likePattern),
            //Last name starts with the given search term

            cb.like(cb.lower(root.<String>get(Contact_.lastName)),
likePattern)
                );
            }

        private String getLikePattern(final String searchTerm) {
            return searchTerm.toLowerCase() + "%";
            }
        };
    }
}
```

Creating the service method

Our implementation of the `search()` method of the `RepositoryContactService` class contains the following two steps:

1. We obtain the `Specification<Contact>` object by using our specification builder.
2. We get the search results by calling the `findAll()` method of the repository and passing the `Specification<Contact>` object as a parameter.

The source code of our implementation is given as follows:

```
@Transactional(readOnly = true)
@Override
public List<Contact> search(String searchTerm) {
    Specification<Contact> contactSpec = firstOrLastNameStartsWith(sea
rchTerm);
    return repository.findAll(contactSpec);
}
```

Pros and cons

We have now learned how we can implement dynamic queries by using the JPA Criteria API. Before we can use these skills in real-world applications, we should be aware of the pros and cons of this approach. These are described in the following table:

Pros	Cons
• Supports dynamic queries • Syntax verification is done during compilation • Makes it easier to migrate applications using the JPA Criteria API to Spring Data JPA	• Complex queries are hard to implement and understand

Querydsl

Querydsl is a framework that enables the construction of type-safe dynamic queries through an API that resembles SQL (to learn more on Querydsl, visit `http://www.querydsl.com/`). If we want to create queries by using Querydsl, we have to:

1. Configure Querydsl Maven Integration.
2. Generate Querydsl query type.
3. Add Querydsl support to a repository.
4. Create the executed query.
5. Execute the created query.

We will explain these steps in more detail in the following section and we will also take a look of the pros and cons of Querydsl.

Configuring Querydsl-Maven integration

The configuration of the Querydsl-Maven integration consist of two steps:

1. We configure the needed dependencies.
2. We configure the APT Maven plugin that is used for code generation.

Configuring Querydsl Maven dependencies

Because we are using Querydsl with JPA, we have to declare the following dependencies in the `pom.xml` file:

- Querydsl core that provides the core functions of Querydsl
- Querydsl APT, which provides support for APT based code generation
- Querydsl JPA, that adds support for JPA annotations

We are using the Querydsl version 2.8.0. Thus, we have to add the following dependency declarations to the dependencies section of the `pom.xml` file:

```
<dependency>
  <groupId>com.mysema.querydsl</groupId>
  <artifactId>querydsl-core</artifactId>
  <version>2.8.0<version>
</dependency>
<dependency>
  <groupId>com.mysema.querydsl</groupId>
  <artifactId>querydsl-apt</artifactId>
  <version>2.8.0</version>
</dependency>
<dependency>
  <groupId>com.mysema.querydsl</groupId>
  <artifactId>querydsl-jpa</artifactId>
  <version>2.8.0</version>
</dependency>
```

Configuring the code generation Maven plugin

Our next step is to configure the Maven plugin of the Annotation Processing Tool of Java 6, which is used to generate the Querydsl query types. We can configure this plugin by:

1. Configuring the plugin to execute its `process` goal in Maven's `generate-sources` lifecycle phase.
2. Specifying the target directory in which the query types are generated.
3. Configuring the code generator to look for JPA annotations from entity classes.

The configuration of the Maven APT plugin is given as follows:

```
<plugin>
  <groupId>com.mysema.maven</groupId>
    <artifactId>maven-apt-plugin</artifactId>
  <version>1.0.4</version>
  <executions>
      <execution>
          <phase>generate-sources</phase>
      <goals>
        <goal>process</goal>
      </goals>
      <configuration>
        <outputDirectory>target/generated-sources</outputDirectory>
  <processor>com.mysema.query.apt.jpa.JPAAnnotationProcessor</
processor>
      </configuration>
    </execution>
  </executions>
</plugin>
```

Generating Querydsl query types

If our configuration is working properly, Querydsl query types should be generated automatically when we build our project with Maven.

 The Maven APT plugin has a known issue that prevents its usage directly from Eclipse. Eclipse users must create the Querydsl query types manually by running the command mvn generate-sources at command prompt.

The query types are found from the target/generated-sources directory. The following rules will apply for the generated query types:

- Each query type is generated in the same package as the corresponding entity.
- The name of a query type class is built by appending the simple name of the entity class to a letter "Q". For example, since the name of our entity class is Contact, the name of the corresponding Querydsl query type is QContact.

 Before we can use the query types in our code, we must add the target/generated-sources directory as a source directory of our project.

Adding Querydsl support to a repository

We can add Querydsl support to a repository by extending the
`QueryDslPredicateExecutor<T>` interface. When we extend this interface we must
give the type of the managed entity as a type parameter. The source code of the
`ContactRepository` interface is given as follows:

```
public interface ContactRepository extends JpaRepository<Contact,
Long>, QueryDslPredicateExecutor<Contact> {
}
```

After we have extended the `QueryDslPredicateExecutor<T>` interface, we have
access to the following methods:

Method	Description
`long count(Predicate p)`	Returns the number of entities matching with the given search criteria.
`Iterable<Contact> findAll(Predicate p)`	Returns all entities matching with the given search criteria.
`Contact findOne(Predicate p)`	Returns a single entity matching with the given search criteria.

Creating the executed query

Each query must implement the `Predicate` interface that is provided by Querydsl.
Luckily, we don't have to implement this interface manually. Instead, we can use
the query types for creating the actual query objects. A clean way to do this is to
create a special predicate builder class and use a static method for creating the actual
predicates. Let's call this class `ContactPredicates`. Our implementation of the static
method that creates predicates fulfilling the requirements of the search function is
explained as follows:

1. We implement a static `firstOrLastNameStartsWith()` method that returns
   an implementation of the `Predicate` interface.
2. We get a reference to the `QContact` query type.
3. We build our query by using the `QContact` query type.

The source code of our predicate builder class is given as follows:

```
public class ContactPredicates {

    public static Predicate firstOrLastNameStartsWith(final String
searchTerm) {
        QContact contact = QContact.contact;
```

```
       return contact.firstName.startsWithIgnoreCase(searchTerm)
                .or(contact.lastName.startsWithIgnoreCase(searchTe
rm));
    }
}
```

Executing the created query

We have implemented the `search()` method of the `RepositoryContactService` class by:

1. Getting the used predicate by calling the static `firstOrLastNAmeStartsWith()` method of the `ContactPredicates` class.

2. Getting results by calling our repository method and passing the predicate as a parameter.

3. Using the `CollectionUtils` class found from the `Commons Collections` library to add every contact to the returned list.

The source code of our implementation is given as follows:

```
@Transactional(readOnly = true)
@Override
public List<Contact> search(String searchTerm) {
   Predicate contactPredicate = firstOrLastNameStartsWith(searchTerm);

   Iterable<Contact> contacts = repository.findAll(contactPredicate);
   List<Contact> contactList = new ArrayList<Contact>();
   CollectionUtils.addAll(contactList, contacts.iterator());

   return contactList;
}
```

Pros and cons

We are now capable of creating queries by using Spring Data JPA and Querydsl. The pros and cons of Querydsl are described in the following table:

Pros	Cons
• Supports dynamic queries	• Requires code generation
• Clean and understandable API	• Eclipse integration is not working properly
• Syntax verification is done during compilation	

What technique should we use?

In the course of this section, we have been discussing different ways to create queries with Spring Data JPA. We are also aware of the pros and cons of each described technique. This information is refined to concrete guidelines that are given in the following list:

- We should use query methods for creating static queries.

- We can use the query generation from method name strategy if the created query is simple and the method name parser supports the required keywords. Otherwise, we should use the @Query annotation because of its flexibility and because it does not force us to use long and ugly method names.

- Named queries are useful if we cannot create our query method by using the query generation from the method strategy or the @Query annotation. This approach can also be useful if we are migrating an existing application to Spring Data JPA. However, we should use them sparingly when we are creating new applications because they tend to litter our entities with query logic.

- Native queries are useful if we cannot create the query by using the other described techniques or if we need to tune up the performance of an individual query. However, we must understand that using native queries creates a dependency between our application and the used database schema. Also, if we use provider specific SQL extensions, our application is tied to the used database provider.

- We should use the JPA Criteria API for creating dynamic queries if we are migrating an existing application that uses criteria queries to Spring Data JPA. The JPA Criteria API is also a valid option if we cannot live with the problems of the Querydsl-Eclipse integration.

- Querydsl is a great choice for creating dynamic queries. It provides a clean and readable API, which is a huge benefit over the JPA Criteria API. Querydsl should be our first choice for creating dynamic queries from a scratch. The clumsy Eclipse integration is naturally a downside for Eclipse users.

Sorting query results

In the course of this section, we will learn different techniques that can be used to sort query results with Spring Data JPA. We will also learn the guidelines that we can use to select a proper sorting method for each situation.

Sorting with method name

If we are building our queries by using the query generation from the method name strategy, we can sort query results by the following steps:

1. Creating a query method
2. Modifying an existing service method to use the new query method.

Creating the query method

When we are building our queries by using the query generation from the method name strategy, we can use the OrderBy keyword to sort the query results when we:

1. Append the OrderBy keyword to the method name.
2. Append the property expression that corresponds to the property of the entity, which is used to sort the query results, to the method name.
3. Append a keyword describing the sorting order to the method name. If the query results are sorted in ascending order, the keyword Asc should be used. Desc keyword is used when the query results are sorted in descending order.
4. Repeat step 2 and step 3 if more than one property is used to sort the query results.

We can fulfill the new requirement of the search function by appending the string OrderByLastNameAscFirstNameAsc to the name of our query method. The signature of our query method is given as follows:

```
public List<Contact> findByFirstNameStartingWithOrLastNameStartingWith
OrderByLastNameAscFirstNameAsc(String firstName, String lastName);
```

Modifying the service method

We have to modify the search() method of the RepositoryContactService class to delegate the method call forward to the new query method. The source code of this method is given as follows:

```
@Transactional(readOnly = true)
@Override
public List<Contact> search(String searchTerm) {
    return repository.findByFirstNameStartingWithOrLastNameStartingWit
hOrderByLastNameAscFirstNameAsc(searchTerm, searchTerm);
}
```

Sorting with query strings

In some cases, we have to add the sorting logic to the actual query string. If we are using named queries or native queries with the @Query annotation, we must provide the sorting logic in the actual query. It is also possible to add sorting logic to the actual query when we are using @Query annotation with JPQL queries.

JPQL queries

When we want to sort the query results of a JPQL query, we must use the ORDER BY keyword of JPQL. The JPQL query that fulfills the new requirement of the search function is given as follows:

```
SELECT c FROM Contact c WHERE LOWER(c.firstName) LIKE
LOWER(:searchTerm) OR LOWER(c.lastName) LIKE LOWER(:searchTerm) ORDER
BY c.lastName ASC, c.firstName ASC
```

SQL queries

When we want to sort the query results of native SQL queries, we must use the ORDER BY keyword of SQL. The SQL query fulfilling the new requirement of the search function is given as follows:

```
SELECT * FROM contacts c WHERE LOWER(c.first_name) LIKE
LOWER(:searchTerm) OR LOWER(c.last_name) LIKE LOWER(:searchTerm) ORDER
BY c.last_name ASC, c.first_name ASC
```

Sorting with the Sort class

If we are using the methods of the JpaRepository<T, ID> interface, query methods, or the JPA Criteria API, we can use the Sort class for sorting query results. If we decide to use this approach, we have to:

1. Create an instance of the Sort class.

2. Pass the created instance as a parameter to the used repository method.

> We cannot use the Sort class to sort the query results of named queries or native queries declared with @Query annotation.

Since all the techniques that are described later need to get an instance of the `Sort` class, we will have to add a way to create these objects to the `RepositoryContactService` class. We will do this by creating a private `sortByLastNameAndFirstNameAsc()` method. The source code of this method is given as follows:

```
private Sort sortByLastNameAndFirstNameAsc() {
  return new Sort(new Sort.Order(Sort.Direction.ASC, "lastName"),
        new Sort.Order(Sort.Direction.ASC, "firstName")
    );
}
```

JpaRepository

We used the `findAll()` method of the `JpaRepository<T,ID>` interface to get a list of all the entities stored to the database. However, when we extended the `JpaRepository<T,ID>` interface, we also got access to the `List<Contact> findAll(Sort sort)` method which we can use to sort a list of entities that are stored to a database.

As an example, we are going to sort the list of all the entities in ascending order by using last name and first name. We can do this by:

1. Getting a new `Sort` object.
2. Getting the sorted list of entities by calling the `findAll()` method of our repository and passing the created `Sort` object as a parameter.

The source code of the `findAll()` method of the `RepositoryContactService` is given as follows:

```
@Transactional(readOnly = true)
@Override
public List<Contact> findAll() {
  Sort sortSpec = sortByLastNameAndFirstNameAsc();
  return repository.findAll(sortSpec);
}
```

Query generation from the method name

We can also use this approach for sorting the query results of queries that are created by using the query generation from the method name strategy. If we want to use this technique, we have to modify the signature of our query method to take a `Sort` object as a parameter. The signature of our query method, which implements the new sorting requirement of the search function, is given as follows:

```
public Page<Contact> findByFirstNameStartingWithOrLastNameStartingWith
(String firstName, String lastName, Sort sort);
```

Our next step is to change the implementation of the `search()` method of the `RepositoryContactService` class. The new implementation is explained in the following steps:

1. We get a reference to a `Sort` object.
2. We call our new repository method and provide the needed parameters.

The source code of our implementation is given as follows:

```
@Transactional(readOnly = true)
@Override
public List<Contact> search(String searchTerm) {
  Sort sortSpec = sortByLastNameAndFirstNameAsc();
  return repository.findByFirstNameStartingWithOrLastNameStartingWith(
searchTerm, searchTerm, sortSpec);
}
```

@Query annotation

We don't have to add the sorting logic to the actual query if we are using the `@Query` annotation for building queries with JPQL. We can also modify the signature of our query method to take a `Sort` object as a parameter. The declaration of our query method is given as follows:

```
@Query("SELECT c FROM Contact c WHERE LOWER(c.firstName) LIKE
LOWER(:searchTerm) OR LOWER(c.lastName) LIKE LOWER(:searchTerm)")
public Page<Contact> findContacts(@Param("searchTerm") String
searchTerm, Sort sort);
```

The next step is to modify the `search()` method to the `RepositoryContactService` class. Our implementation of this method is described as follows:

1. We create the used like pattern.
2. We get a reference to a `Sort` object.
3. We call our repository method and provide the needed parameters.

The source code of the `search()` method looks like the following code:

```
@Transactional(readOnly = true)
@Override
public List<Contact> search(String searchTerm) {
    String likePattern = buildLikePattern(dto.getSearchTerm());
    Sort sortSpec = sortByLastNameAndFirstNameAsc();
    return repository.findContacts(likePattern, sortSpec);
}
```

JPA Criteria API

In order to create queries by using JPA Criteria API, we had to modify the `ContactRepository` interface to extend the `JpaSpecificationExecutor<T>` interface. This gives us access to the `List<Contact> findAll(Specification spec, Sort sort)` method that returns a sorted list of entities matching the given search conditions.

Our implementation of the `search()` method of the `RepositoryContactService` class is described as follows:

1. We get the used search criteria by using our specification builder class.

2. We get the used `Sort` object.

3. We will call the `findAll()` method of the `ContactRepository` and provide the necessary parameters.

Our `search()` method is given as follows:

```
@Transactional(readOnly = true)
@Override
public List<Contact> search(String searchTerm) {
    Specification<Contact> contactSpec = firstOrLastNameStartsWith(se
archTerm);
    Sort sortSpec = sortByLastNameAndFirstNameAsc();
    return repository.findAll(contactSpec, sortSpec);
}
```

Sorting with Querydsl

Extending the `QuerydslPredicateExecutor<T>` interface in our contact repository gave us access to the `Iterable<Contact> findAll(Predicate predicate, OrderSpecifier<?>... orders)` method that returns a sorted list of all entities that match with the given search criteria.

First, we must create a service method that creates an array of `OrderSpecifier` objects. The source code of the `sortByLastNameAndFirstNameAsc()` method is given as follows:

```
private OrderSpecifier[] sortByLastNameAndFirstNameAsc() {
   OrderSpecifier[] orders = {QContact.contact.lastName.asc(),
QContact.contact.firstName.asc()};
   return orders;
}
```

Our next step is to modify the implementation of the `search()` method of the `RepositoryContactService` class to fulfill the given requirements. Our implementation of the `search()` method is described as follows:

1. We get the used search criteria.
2. We get the used `OrderSpecifier` array by calling the `sortByLastNameAndFirstNameAsc()` method that we created earlier.
3. We call the `findAll()` method of the `ContactRepository` and provide the needed parameters.
4. We use the `CollectionUtils` class found from the `Commons Collections` library to add all contacts to the returned list.

The source code of the `search()` method is given as follows:

```
@Transactional(readOnly = true)
@Override
public List<Contact> search(String searchTerm) {
   Predicate contactPredicate = firstOrLastNameStartsWith(searchTerm);
   OrderSpecifier[] orderSpecs = sortByLastNameAndFirstNameAsc();

   Iterable<Contact> contacts = repository.findAll(contactPredicate,
orderSpecs);
   List<Contact> contactList = new ArrayList<Contact>();
   CollectionUtils.addAll(contactList, contacts.iterator());

   return contactList;
}
```

What technique should we use?

The best approach is to keep the query generation and sorting logic in the same place, if possible. In this way, we can check the implementation of our query by looking at one place, and one place only. This general guideline can be refined to the following concrete instructions:

- If we are using the query generation from the method name, we should use this approach for sorting the query results. If the method name becomes too long or ugly, we can always use the `Sort` class for sorting our query results but this should not be our first choice. Instead, we should consider building our query by using the `@Query` annotation.

- If we are using JPQL or SQL, we should add the sorting logic in our query string. This way we can check our query logic and sorting logic from the same place.

- If we are using named queries or native queries with the `@Query` annotation, we must add the sorting logic into our query string.

- When we are building our queries by using the JPA Criteria API, we must use the `Sort` class because that is only the method provided by the `JpaSpecificationExecutor<T>` interface.

- When we are using Querydsl for building our queries, we must use the `OrderSpecifier` class to sort our query results because that is required by the `QueryDslPredicateExecutor<T>` interface.

Paginating query results

Paginating query results is a very common requirement for practically every application that presents some kind of data. The key component of the pagination support of Spring Data JPA is the `Pageable` interface that declares the following methods:

Method	Description
int getPageNumber()	Returns the number of the requested page. The page numbers are zero indexed. Thus, the number of the first page is zero.
int getPageSize()	Returns the number of elements shown on a single page. The page size must always be larger than zero.
int getOffset()	Returns the selected offset according to the given page number and page size.
Sort getSort()	Returns the sorting parameters used to sort the query results.

We can use this interface to paginate the query results with Spring Data JPA by:

1. Creating a new `PageRequest` object. We can use the `PageRequest` class because it implements the `Pageable` interface.

2. Passing the created object to a repository method as a parameter.

If we are using query methods for creating our queries, we have got two options for the return type of the query method:

- If we need to access the metadata of the requested page, we can make our query method return `Page<T>` where `T` is the type of the managed entity.

- If we are interested in only getting the contacts of the requested page, we should make our query method return `List<T>`, where `T` is the type of the managed entity.

In order to add pagination to our contact manager application, we have to make changes to the service layer of our application and implement the pagination. Both of these tasks are described in more detail in the following subsections.

Changing the service layer

Since the Spring Data JPA repositories are just interfaces, we have to create the `PageRequest` objects on the service layer. This means that we have to figure out a way to pass the pagination parameters to the service layer and use these parameters to create the `PageRequest` object. We can achieve this goal by following these steps:

1. We create a class that stores the pagination parameters and the search term.

2. We change the method signatures of the service interface.

3. We implement a way to create `PageRequest` objects.

Creating a class for pagination parameters

First, we have to create a class that is used to store both the pagination parameters and the used search term. Spring Data provides a custom argument resolver called `PageableArgumentResolver` that will automatically build the `PageRequest` object by parsing the request parameters. More information about this approach is available at `http://static.springsource.org/spring-data/data-jpa/docs/current/reference/html/#web-pagination`.

We will not use this approach since we don't want to introduce a dependency between our web layer and Spring Data. Instead we will use a simple DTO that has only a few fields, and getters and setters. The source code of the SearchDTO is given as follows:

```
public class SearchDTO {

    private int pageIndex;
    private int pageSize;
    private String searchTerm;

    //Getters and Setters
}
```

Changing the service interface

We need to change the ContactService interface of our example application in order to provide pagination support for both the contact list and the search result list. The required changes are mentioned as follows:

- We have to replace the findAll() method with findAllForPage() method that takes the page number and the page size as a parameter
- We have to modify the signature of the search() method to take SearchDTO as a parameter

The signatures of changed methods are given as follows:

```
public List<Contact> findAllForPage(int pageIndex, int pageSize);

public List<Contact> search(SearchDTO dto);
```

Creating PageRequest objects

Before we can move forward to the actual implementations we have to add a new method to the RepositoryContactService class. This method is used to create PageRequest objects that are passed as a parameter to our repository. The implementation of the buildPageSpecification() method is explained as follows:

1. We use the sortByLastNameAndFirstNameAsc() method to get a reference to the used Sort object.
2. We use the page number, page size, and the Sort object to create a new PageRequest object.

The source code of the relevant methods is given as follows:

```
private Pageable buildPageSpecification(int pageIndex, int pageSize) {
  Sort sortSpec = sortByLastNameAndFirstNameAsc();
  return new PageRequest(pageIndex, pageSize, sortSpec);
}

private Sort sortByLastNameAndFirstNameAsc() {
  return new Sort(new Sort.Order(Sort.Direction.ASC, "lastName"),
      new Sort.Order(Sort.Direction.ASC, "firstName")
    );
}
```

Implementing pagination

In order to paginate the results of our queries, we have to pass the created `PageRequest` object to a correct repository method. This method depends on the approach, which we are using to build our queries. Each of these approaches is described in this subsection.

JpaRepository

Because the `ContactRepository` extends the `JpaRepository<T, ID>` interface, we got access to the `Page<Contact> findAll(Pageable page)` method that we can use to paginate the list of all entities. The implementation of the `findAllForPage()` method of the `RepositoryContactService` class is described as follows:

1. We get the used `PageRequest` object.
2. We get a reference to `Page<Contact>` by calling the repository method and passing the `PageRequest` object as parameter.
3. We return a list of contacts.

The source code of our `findAllForPage()` method is given as follows:

```
@Transactional(readOnly = true)
@Override
public List<Contact> findAllForPage(int pageIndex, int pageSize) {
  Pageable pageSpecification = buildPageSpecification(pageIndex,
pageSize);

  Page<Contact> page = repository.findAll(pageSpecification);

  return page.getContent();
}
```

Query generation from the method name

If we are building our queries by using the query generation from the method name strategy, we can paginate query results by:

1. Adding pagination support to the query method.
2. Calling the query method from a service method.

Adding pagination support to the query method

Adding pagination support to our query method is rather simple. All we have to do is make the following changes to the signature of the query method:

1. Add the `Pageable` interface as a parameter of the query method.
2. Determine the return type of the query method.

Since we are not interested in the page metadata, the signature of our query method is given as follows:

```
public List<Contact> findByFirstNameStartingWithOrLastNameStartingWith
(String firstName, String lastName, Pageable page);
```

Modifying the service class

The modifications needed by the `search()` method of the `RepositoryContactService` are rather simple. We get a reference to a `PageRequest` object and pass it as a parameter to our query method. The source code of the modified method is given as follows:

```
@Transactional(readOnly = true)
@Override
public List<Contact> search(SearchDTO dto) {
    Pageable pageSpecification = buildPageSpecification(dto.
getPageIndex(), dto.getPageSize());

    return repository.findByFirstNameStartingWithOrLastNameStartingWit
h(dto.getSearchTerm(), dto.getSearchTerm(), pageSpecification);
}
```

Named queries

If we want to paginate the query results of named queries, we have to:

1. Add pagination support to the query method.
2. Call the query method from a service method.

Adding pagination support to the query method

We can add pagination support to a query method that is backed up by a named query by adding the `Pageable` interface as a parameter of the query method. At this point we do not need the page metadata for anything. Thus, the signature of our query method is given as follows:

```
public List<Contact> findContacts(@Param("searchTerm") String
searchTerm, Pageable page);
```

Modifying the service class

Our implementation of the `search()` method of the `RepositoryContactService` class is explained as follows:

1. We get the used like pattern.
2. We get the required `PageRequest` object.
3. We get the list of contacts by calling the modified query method.

The source code of our modified `search()` method is given as follows:

```
@Transactional(readOnly = true)
@Override
public List<Contact> search(SearchDTO dto) {
    String likePattern = buildLikePattern(dto.getSearchTerm());

    Pageable pageSpecification = buildPageSpecification(dto.
getPageIndex(), dto.getPageSize());

    return repository.findContacts(likePattern, pageSpecification);
}
```

@Query annotation

We can paginate the query results of JPQL queries built with the `@Query` annotation by:

1. Adding the pagination support to a query method.
2. Calling the query method from a service method.

Adding pagination support to a query method

We can add pagination support to a query method that is annotated with the `@Query` annotation by making the following changes to its signature:

1. We add the `Pageable` interface as a parameter of the method.
2. We determine the return type of the method.

At this point we are not interested in the metadata of the returned page. Thus, the declaration of the query method is given as follows:

```
@Query("SELECT c FROM Contact c WHERE LOWER(c.firstName) LIKE
LOWER(:searchTerm) OR LOWER(c.lastName) LIKE LOWER(:searchTerm)")
public List<Contact> findContacts(@Param("searchTerm") String
searchTerm, Pageable page);
```

Modifying the service method

The implementation of the `search()` method of the `RepositoryContactService` class is described as follows:

1. We get the used like pattern.
2. We get a reference to the used `PageRequest` object.
3. We get the list of contacts by calling the query method and passing the like pattern and the created `PageRequest` object as a parameter.

The source code of the `search()` method is given as follows:

```
@Transactional(readOnly = true)
@Override
public List<Contact> search(SearchDTO dto) {
    String likePattern = buildLikePattern(dto.getSearchTerm());

    Pageable pageSpecification = buildPageSpecification(dto.
getPageIndex(), dto.getPageSize());

    return repository.findContacts(likePattern, pageSpecification);
}
```

JPA Criteria API

In order to build queries with the JPA Criteria API, the `ContactRepository` interface must extend the `JpaSpecificationExecutor<T>` interface. This gives us access to the `Page<Contact> findAll(Specification spec, Pageable page)` method that can be used to paginate the query results of criteria queries. The only thing that is left for us to do is to modify the `search()` method of the `RepositoryContactService` class. Our implementation is explained as follows:

1. We get the used specification.
2. We get the used `PageRequest` object.
3. We get the `Page` implementation by calling the repository method and passing the specification and the `PageRequest` object as a parameter.
4. We return the requested list of contacts by calling the `getContent()` method of the `Page` class.

The source code of our search method is given as follows:

```
@Transactional(readOnly = true)
@Override
public List<Contact> search(SearchDTO dto) {
    Specification<Contact> contactSpec =
firstOrLastNameStartsWith(dto.getSearchTerm());
    Pageable pageSpecification = buildPageSpecification(dto.
getPageIndex(), dto.getPageSize());

    Page<Contact> page = repository.findAll(contactSpec,
pageSpecification);

    return page.getContent();
}
```

Querydsl

Since the `ContactRepository` interface extends the `QueryDslPredicateExecutor<T>` interface, we got access to the `Page<Contact> findAll(Predicate predicate, Pageable page)` method that we can use to paginate query results. In order to add pagination support to our search function, we have to make some changes to the existing `search()` method of the `RepositoryContactService` class. The new implementation of this method is described in the following steps:

1. We get a reference to the used `Predicate`.
2. We get the used `PageRequest` object.

3. We get a `Page` reference by calling the repository method and passing the `Predicate` and `PageRequest` object as parameters.

4. We return the requested contacts.

The source code of our new `search()` method looks like the following code:

```
@Transactional(readOnly = true)
@Override
public List<Contact> search(SearchDTO dto) {
    Predicate contactPredicate = firstOrLastNameStartsWith(dto.
getSearchTerm());
    Pageable pageSpecification = buildPageSpecification(dto.
getPageIndex(), dto.getPageSize());

    Page<Contact> page = repository.findAll(contactPredicate,
pageSpecification);

    return page.getContent();
}
```

Summary

In this chapter, we have learned that:

- We can use query generation from method name, named queries, or the @Query annotation for the purpose of creating query methods with Spring Data JPA
- We can create dynamic queries by using either JPA Criteria API or Querydsl
- There are three different methods we can use to sort query results
- If we are paginating the query results of a query method, the return type of the method can be either List or Page
- Each query creation method has its strengths and weaknesses that we must consider when we are selecting the correct solution for the current problem

Sometimes we need to add custom functions to our repositories. This issue is addressed in the next chapter.

4
Adding Custom Functionality to JPA Repositories

We have learned how we can manage our entities and create database queries with Spring Data JPA. We have also learned how we can sort and paginate query results. However, if we take a purist architectural point of view, we notice that the described solutions are not following the **separation of concerns** principle. In fact, our service layer contains code that reveals the inner workings of our repository layer.

This is a trade off between architectural purity and productivity. As always, this choice has some consequences. If we have to migrate our application away from Spring Data JPA, we have to make changes to both the service and repository layer. However, how many times have we heard that the repository layer of an application has to be changed so radically? Exactly. These situations are very rare. Thus, this risk is worth taking when the reward is high.

The techniques described in this chapter can be used to hide the implementation specific details from our service layer but they have other applications as well. In this chapter, we will cover the following topics:

- How we can add custom functionality to a single repository
- How we can add custom functionality to all repositories

We will use the Querydsl example application created in Chapter 3, *Building Queries with Spring Data JPA*, as a starting point. Let's first refresh our memory and spend a moment to review the structure of our example application. Our service layer consists of a single class called `RepositoryPersonService` that uses our repository interface called `ContactRepository`. The pagination and query building logic of our application is located at the service layer. This situation is illustrated in the following diagram:

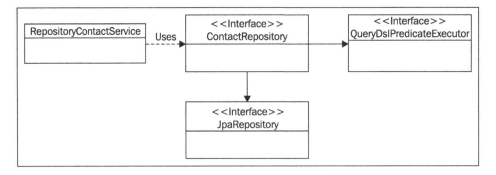

Adding custom functionality to a single repository

The ability to add custom functionality to a single repository is a useful feature when the added functionality is related only to a single entity. In this section, we will investigate how this can be done, and move the pagination and search logic from the service layer to the repository layer.

If we want to add custom functionality to a single repository, we have to follow the following steps:

1. Create a custom interface that declares the custom methods.
2. Implement the created interface.
3. Create a repository interface.
4. Create a service implementation that uses the custom functionality.

Creating the custom interface

Our first step is to create an interface that declares the custom repository methods. Since our goal is to move the pagination and search logic to the repository layer, we have to add the following methods to the created interface:

Method	Description
`List<Contact> findAllForPage(int pageIndex, int pageSize)`	Returns all contacts belonging to the requested page.
`List<Contact> findContactsForPage(String searchTerm, int pageIndex, int pageSize)`	Returns all contacts that match with the given search term and belong to the requested page.

The source code of the `PaginatingContactRepository` interface is given as follows:

```
public interface PaginatingContactRepository {

    public List<Contact> findAllForPage(int pageIndex, int pageSize);

    public List<Contact> findContactsForPage(String searchTerm, int pageIndex, int pageSize);
}
```

Implementing the created interface

We have now created an interface that specifies our custom repository methods. Our next step is to create an implementation of this interface and move all pagination and query building code from the service layer to this class.

The repository infrastructure looks for the implementation of our custom interface from the same package where the interface is located. It is looking for a class, with name matching to a string that is created by appending a suffix to the simple name of the actual repository interface. By default the value of this suffix is `Impl`.

 We can set the suffix by using either the `repository-impl-postfix` attribute of Spring Data JPA's `repositories` namespace element or the `repositoryImplementationPostfix` property of the `@EnableJpaRepositories` annotation.

At the moment we are perfectly happy with the default suffix. Thus, the name of the class that implements our custom interface must be `ContactRepositoryImpl`. We can implement this class by following these steps:

1. Write some plumbing code needed to configure the `QueryDslJpaRepository<T, ID>` class that is used to execute our queries.

2. Implement the methods declared in our custom interface.

Configuring the repository class

In this phase we will write the code that is needed to obtain an instance of the `QueryDslJpaRepository<Contact, Long>` class. This process has the following steps:

1. Use the `@PersistenceContext` annotation to get a reference to the used entity manager.

2. Create an `init()` method and annotate it with the `@PostConstruct` annotation. This ensures that the method called after the bean has been constructed and the entity manager reference is injected.

3. Implement the `init()` method and create a new `QueryDslJpaRepository<Contact, Long>` object.

The source code of our implementation is given as follows:

```
public class ContactRepositoryImpl implements
PaginatingContactRepository {

    @PersistenceContext
    private EntityManager entityManager;

    private QueryDslJpaRepository<Contact, Long> repository;

    //Add methods here

    @PostConstruct
    public void init() {
        JpaEntityInformation<Contact, Long> contactEntityInfo =
new JpaMetamodelEntityInformation<Contact, Long>(Contact.class,
entityManager.getMetamodel());
        repository = new QueryDslJpaRepository<Contact,
Long>(contactEntityInfo, entityManager);
    }
}
```

Implementing the custom methods

At the moment the created class cannot be compiled because we have not implemented the custom methods yet. Also, before we can implement these methods, we have to move the pagination logic from the service layer to the ContactRepositoryImpl class. Thus, this process has the following two steps:

1. Add the pagination related code to our repository implementation.
2. Implement the custom repository methods.

First, we have to add the pagination related code to our repository. This means that we have to add both the sortByLastNameAndFirstNameAsc() and buildPageSpecification() methods to the ContactRepositoryImpl class. The implementations of these methods remain unchanged as we can see in the following code:

```
private Pageable buildPageSpecification(int pageIndex, int pageSize) {
   return new PageRequest(pageIndex, pageSize,
sortByLastNameAndFirstNameAsc());
}

private Sort sortByLastNameAndFirstNameAsc() {
   return new Sort(new Sort.Order(Sort.Direction.ASC, "lastName"),
        new Sort.Order(Sort.Direction.ASC, "firstName")
   );
}
```

The next step is to write an implementation for the findAllForPage() method that is used to get a list of contacts belonging to a requested page. This means that we have to:

1. Get a page specification by using the private buildPageSpecification() method.
2. Get the contents of the requested page by calling the findAll() method of the repository and passing the page specification as a parameter.
3. Return a list of contacts.

The source code of the findAllForPage() method is given as follows:

```
@Override
public List<Contact> findAllForPage(int pageIndex, int pageSize) {
    Pageable pageSpec = buildPageSpecification(pageIndex, pageSize);
    Page wanted = repository.findAll(pageSpec);

    return wanted.getContent();
}
```

Our last task is to provide an implementation for the findContactsForPage() method. The implementation of this method has the following steps:

1. Get the used search condition by calling the static firstOrLastNameStartsWith() method of the ContactPredicates class.

2. Get the page specification by calling the private buildPageSpecification() method.

3. Get the contents of the requested page by calling the findAll() method of the repository and providing the necessary parameters.

4. Return a list of contacts.

The source code of the findContactsForPage() method is given as follows:

```
@Override
public List<Contact> findContactsForPage(String searchTerm, int
pageIndex, int pageSize) {
    Predicate searchCondition = firstOrLastNameStartsWith(searchTerm);
    Pageable pageSpec = buildPageSpecification(pageIndex, pageSize);
    Page wanted = repository.findAll(searchCondition, pageSpec);

    return wanted.getContent();
}
```

Creating the repository interface

We have now implemented the custom functionality and it is time to add this functionality to our repository. We have to make two changes to the existing ContactRepository interface. They are as follows:

1. We can make the custom methods available to the users of our repository by extending the PaginatingContactRepository interface.

2. Because the service layer has no need for the specific methods from the Querydsl library anymore, we can remove the QueryDslPredicateExecutor interface from the list of extended interfaces.

The source code of our new repository interface is given as follows:

```
public interface ContactRepository extends JpaRepository<Contact,
Long>, PaginatingContactRepository {
}
```

Creating the service implementation

The last step is to modify the `RepositoryContactService` class to use the custom functionality. This step has the following two phases:

1. Remove the `buildPageSpecification()` and `sortByLastNameAndFirstNameAsc()` methods.

2. Modify the `findAllForPage()` and `search()` methods to delegate the method call forward to our repository.

The source code of the modified methods is given as follows:

```
@Transactional(readOnly = true)
@Override
public List<Contact> findAllForPage(int pageIndex, int pageSize) {
    return repository.findAllForPage(pageIndex, pageSize);
}

@Transactional(readOnly = true)
@Override
public List<Contact> search(SearchDTO dto) {
    return repository.findContactsForPage(dto.getSearchTerm(), dto.
getPageIndex(), dto.getPageSize());
}
```

What did we just do?

We just moved the pagination and search logic from the `RepositoryContactService` class to the `ContactRepositoryImpl` class and eliminated the dependency between our service layer and Querydsl. The outcome of our actions is illustrated in the following diagram:

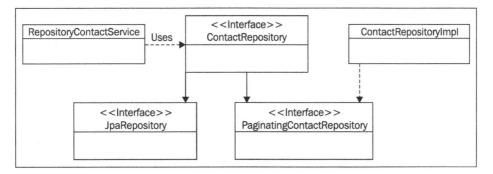

Adding custom functionality to all repositories

Sometimes we have to add custom functionality to all repositories. In this section, we will learn how we can do this and create a custom repository method that is used to delete an entity by using its ID.

We can add custom functionality to all repositories by following these steps:

1. Create a base interface that declares the custom methods.
2. Implement the created interface.
3. Create a repository factory bean.
4. Configure Spring Data JPA to use our repository factory bean.
5. Create a repository interface.
6. Implement a service class that uses the custom functionality.

Creating the base repository interface

We start by creating a base repository interface that declares the methods that are available in the actual repositories. We can do this by:

1. Creating an interface that takes the type of the managed entity and the type of its ID as a type parameter.
2. Extending both the `JpaRepository<T, ID>` and `QueryDslPredicateExecutor<T>` interfaces in our base repository interface.
3. Annotating the interface with the `@NoRepositoryBean` annotation. This ensures that Spring Data JPA does not create a repository implementation for this interface. Another solution is to move this interface from the repository base package, but since it is often hard to find a logical place for it, we will not do it.
4. Adding a `T deleteById(ID id)` method to this interface. This method returns the deleted entity, and it throws `NotFoundException` if no entity is found with the ID that is given as a parameter.

Let's call this interface `BaseRepository`. Its source code is given as follows:

```
@NoRepositoryBean
public interface BaseRepository<T, ID extends Serializable> extends
JpaRepository<T, ID>, QueryDslPredicateExecutor<T> {

    public T deleteById(ID id) throws NotFoundException;
}
```

Implementing the base repository interface

Next we have to write an implementation of the `BaseRepository<T, ID>` interface. This process includes the following steps:

1. Create a class that implements the `BaseRepository<T, ID>` interface and extends the `QueryDslJpaRepository<T, ID>` class. This ensures that the class has access to the methods provided by the `JpaRepository<T, ID>` interface and that Querydsl can be used.

2. Add a constructor that is used to simply pass the needed information forward to the superclass.

3. Implement the `deleteById()` method. First, this method obtains the deleted entity. If an entity is not found, this method throws `NotFoundException`. Otherwise this method deletes the found entity and returns the deleted entity.

The source code of the created `GenericBaseRepository` class is given as follows:

```
public class GenericBaseRepository<T, ID extends Serializable> extends
QueryDslJpaRepository<T, ID> implements BaseRepository<T, ID> {

    public GenericBaseRepository(JpaEntityInformation<T, ID>
entityMetadata, EntityManager entityManager) {
        super(entityMetadata, entityManager);
    }

    @Override
    public T deleteById(ID id) throws NotFoundException {
        T deleted = findOne(id);
        if (deleted == null) {
            throw new NotFoundException();
```

```
        }

        delete(deleted);
        return deleted;
    }
}
```

Creating the repository factory bean

Now that we have implemented the custom functionality, we have to ensure that it is used when the concrete repository implementations are created. This means that we have to create a custom repository factory bean that replaces the default repository factory bean. Our repository factory bean has a single purpose: It will provide GenericBaseRepository as an implementation of all interfaces extending the Repository interface. We can create a custom repository factory bean by following these steps:

1. Create a skeleton of the repository factory bean class.
2. Create a repository factory class.
3. Create a builder method used to build new repository factories.

Creating the skeleton of the repository factory bean class

First we have to create the repository factory bean class. This class must extend the JpaRepositoryFactoryBean<R, T, I> class that is the default repository factory bean of Spring Data JPA. This class has three type parameters: the type of the repository, the type of the entity, and the type of the entity's ID. The source code of the class skeleton is given as follows:

```
public class BaseRepositoryFactoryBean <R extends JpaRepository<T, I>,
T, I extends Serializable> extends JpaRepositoryFactoryBean<R, T, I> {

}
```

Creating the repository factory inner class

The second step is to create the actual repository factory class. The implementation of this class includes the following steps:

1. Add the BaseRepositoryFactory class as a protected inner class to the BaseRepositoryFactoryBean class.

2. Make the created class extend the `JpaRepositoryFactory` class.

3. Override the `getTargetRepository()` method of the `JpaRepositoryFactory` class. This method is responsible for creating the actual repository implementations.

4. Override the `getRepositoryBaseClass()` method of the `JpaRepositoryFactory` class, which simply returns the class of the base repository implementation. We can ignore the metadata given as a parameter because that information is used by the `JpaRepositoryFactory` to decide whether it should return the `SimpleJpaRepository` or `QueryDslJpaRepository` class.

The source code of the repository factory inner class is given as follows:

```
protected static class BaseRepositoryFactory<T, I extends
Serializable> extends JpaRepositoryFactory {

  private EntityManager entityManager;

  public BaseRepositoryFactory(EntityManager entityManager) {
    super(entityManager);
      this.entityManager = entityManager;
  }

  @Override
  protected Object getTargetRepository(RepositoryMetadata metadata)
{
      return new GenericBaseRepository<T,
I>((JpaEntityInformation<T,I>) getEntityInformation(metadata.
getDomainType()), entityManager);
  }

  @Override
  protected Class<?> getRepositoryBaseClass(RepositoryMetadata
metadata) {
      return GenericBaseRepository.class;
  }
}
```

Creating the builder method for the repository factory

We can create new instances of our custom repository factory class by overriding the createRepositoryFactory() method of the JpaRepositoryFactoryBean class in the BaseRepositoryFactoryBean class. This method simply creates a new instance of the BaseRepositoryFactory class and passes an entity manager reference as a constructor parameter. The source code of the overridden method is given as follows:

```
@Override
protected RepositoryFactorySupport createRepositoryFactory(EntityManag
er entityManager) {
    return new BaseRepositoryFactory(entityManager);
}
```

Configuring Spring Data JPA

Next we have to configure Spring Data JPA to use the custom repository factory bean when it is creating concrete implementations of repository interfaces. We can do this by using the repositoryFactoryBeanClass property of the @EnableJpaRepositories annotation. In other words, we have to add the following annotation to the ApplicationContext class:

```
@EnableJpaRepositories(basePackages - {"com.packtpub.springdata.jpa.
repository"}, repositoryFactoryBeanClass = BaseRepositoryFactoryBean.
class)
```

 If we are using XML to configure our application, we can use the factory-class attribute of Spring Data JPA's repositories namespace element.

Creating the repository interface

We have now made the custom functionality available to all repositories. Now we have to create a repository interface for the Contact entity. We can do this by following these steps:

1. Remove the JpaRepository and the QueryDslPredicateExecutor interfaces from the list of extended interfaces.

2. Extend the BaseRepository<T, ID> interface.

The source code of the `ContactRepository` interface is given as follows:

```
public interface ContactRepository extends BaseRepository<Contact,
Long> {
}
```

Implementing the service layer

Because the old implementation of the `delete()` method of the `RepositoryContactService` class contained the same functionality as our new `deleteById()` repository method, we have to change the `delete()` method of the `RepositoryContactService` class to delegate the method call forward to the new repository method. The source code of our new `delete()` method is given as follows:

```
@Transactional(rollbackFor = NotFoundException.class)
@Override
public Contact deleteById(Long id) throws NotFoundException {
    return repository.deleteById(id);
}
```

What did we just do?

We implemented a generic delete method that is automatically available to all repositories of our application. This eliminates the need to add entity specific delete logic to the service layer and reduces code duplication. We also created a custom repository factory that provides `GenericBaseRepository` as an implementation for our repository interface. The result of our work is illustrated in the following diagram:

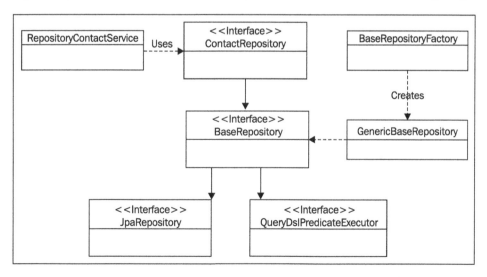

Summary

In this chapter, we have learned that we can add custom functionality either to a single repository or to all repositories. However, this chapter also had another very important lesson. We noticed that adding custom functionality to repositories increases the complexity of our application and forces us to write boilerplate code that can be cumbersome to both implement and maintain. That is why we should use the techniques described in this chapter only when it is absolutely necessary.

This was the last chapter that describes the usage of Spring Data JPA. In the next chapter, we will learn how we can install Redis on a computer that runs a Unix-like operating system and set up a web application project that uses Redis as a data storage.

5
Getting Started with Spring Data Redis

Before the Spring Data Redis project was born, a normal way to communicate with Redis was to use client libraries that can be compared to the JDBC drivers of relational databases. The difference is that these clients do not implement a standard API that makes it hard to switch from one connector to another. Obviously, the million-dollar question is, how can Spring Data Redis make our life easier?

Spring Data Redis hides the APIs of different client libraries behind a single API that is clean and easy to use. In theory, this ensures that we can change the used Redis connector without making any changes to our application. Even though this is indeed a useful feature if we have to change the used connector, it would be naive to claim that we should start using Spring Data Redis only because of this feature. We have to remember that we will most likely stick with one Redis connector throughout the life cycle of our application.

However, we must remember that applications are basically built by combining different components together. Spring Data Redis provides a seamless integration with the Spring framework that is a popular tool used to create enterprise applications. This is naturally a huge benefit for any developer who is writing a Spring-powered application that uses Redis.

[More information about Spring Data Redis and its features can be found at `http://www.springsource.org/spring-data/redis/`.]

This chapter will guide us through the initial configuration phase and help us to set up a web application project that uses Spring Data Redis. In this chapter, we will cover the following topics:

- How we can install Redis to a computer running a Unix-like operating system
- How we can get the required dependencies of Spring Data Redis by using Maven
- How we can configure the application context of our application by using programmatic configuration
- How we can configure our Redis connection in an application context configuration class

Installing Redis

Spring Data Redis requires that Redis 2.0 or above is used, and it recommends that Redis 2.2 is used. However, it is possible to use newer Redis versions even though the new features might not be supported yet. This book assumes that we are using Redis version 2.6.0-rc6.

At the moment Redis does not officially support Windows but there are some unofficial ports available. If you want to install Redis to a Windows computer, download one of the unofficial source packages and follow its installation instructions. The download links of the unofficial Windows ports are available at http://redis.io/download.

 The only dependencies of Redis are a working GCC compiler and libc. The best way to install these dependencies is to use the package manager of the used Linux distribution. If Redis is compiled on a computer that uses an OS X operating system, one should ensure that both Xcode and its command line tools are installed.

We can install Redis to a computer running a Unix-like operating system by following these steps:

1. Download the Redis source package. We use a command line utility called wget for retrieving the source package.
2. Decompress the source package.
3. Compile Redis.

We can finish the installation procedure by running these commands at the command line:

```
wget http://redis.googlecode.com/files/redis-2.6.0-rc6.tar.gz
tar xzf redis-2.6.0-rc6.tar.gz
cd redis-2.6.0-rc6
make
```

 At the moment the source packages are hosted on Google Code. If the packages are moved to a different host or if a different Redis version is installed, these commands must be modified accordingly.

After the compilation has finished successfully, we can start our Redis server by running the following command at the command prompt:

```
./src/redis-server
```

If our installation was successful, we should see the output as shown in the following screenshot:

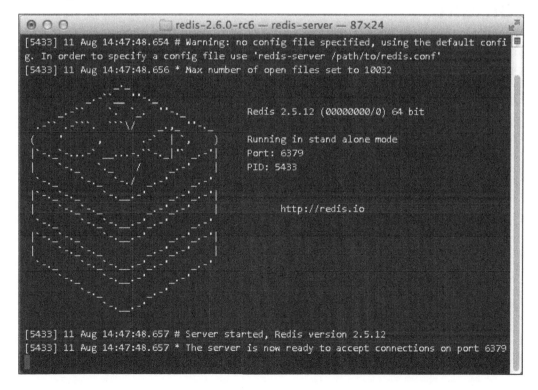

The official Redis homepage has a comprehensive documentation that offers more information about the usage and configuration of Redis. This documentation is available at `http://redis.io/documentation`.

Getting the required dependencies

Getting the dependencies required by Spring Data Redis is rather easy. The only dependency that is required is Spring Data Redis, and we can get it by adding the following dependency declaration to the `pom.xml` file:

```xml
<dependency>
  <groupId>org.springframework.data</groupId>
  <artifactId>spring-data-redis</artifactId>
  <version>1.0.1.RELEASE</version>
</dependency>
```

Configuring the Spring application context

We will use the Java configuration for configuring the application context of our application. The name of our application context configuration class is `ApplicationContext`, and its implementation is explained in the following points:

1. The `@Configuration` annotation is used to identify the class as an application context configuration class.

2. The `@ComponentScan` annotation is used to configure the base package of our controllers.

3. The `@EnableWebMvc` annotation is used to enable the Spring MVC.

4. The values of the configuration parameters are fetched from a property file that is imported by using the `@PropertySource` annotation. The `Environment` interface is used to access the property values stored in this file.

5. The `redisConnectionFactory()` method is used to configure the Redis connection factory bean. The implementation of this method depends on the used Redis connector.

The source code of our application context configuration skeleton class is given as follows:

```
@Configuration
@ComponentScan(basePackages = {
        "com.packtpub.springdata.redis.controller"
})
@EnableWebMvc
@PropertySource("classpath:application.properties")
public class ApplicationContext extends WebMvcConfigurerAdapter {

    @Resource
    private Environment env;

    @Bean
    public RedisConnectionFactory redisConnectionFactory() {
      //Add implementation
    }

    //Add other configuration here
}
```

The contents of the `application.properties` file are as follows:

```
redis.host = localhost
redis.port = 6379
```

Configuring the Redis connection

Spring Data Redis supports four different connectors that can be used to interact with a Redis server. These connectors are described in the following table:

Connector	Description
Jedis	Jedis is a Redis connector that is fully compatible with Redis 2.0.0 commands. The project is hosted at GitHub, and more information about this found at `https://github.com/xetorthio/jedis`.
JRedis	JRedis is a Redis connector that does not yet have official support for Redis 2.x. However, it is possible to use a forked version of this library that adds support for Redis 2.x. The forked version of the JRedis library is hosted at GitHub, and its homepage is found at `https://github.com/anthonylauzon/jredis`.

Connector	Description
RJC	RJC is a Redis connector that is compatible with Redis 2.X. More information about the RJC connector is found at `https://github.com/e-mzungu/rjc`.
SRP	SRP is a Redis connector that supports Redis 2.6 commands. The project's homepage is found at `https://github.com/spullara/redis-protocol`.

Unfortunately, at the moment some of the supported connectors are at the early stage of development and they do not support all the available features of Redis. If the underlying connector does not support the performed operation, the exception, `UnsupportedOperationException`, is thrown.

Also, the configuration options that we can use with Spring Data Redis depend on the used connector. The following table describes differences between the supported Redis connectors (X means that the configuration option is supported and - means that it is not):

Connector	Password	Connection Pool
Jedis	X	X
JRedis	X	X
RJC	X	X
SRP	-	-

Jedis is the default connector of Spring Data Redis and at the moment it should be our first choice because it is the most mature of the supported connectors and it is being actively developed. However, we will take a look at the configuration process of each supported connector because the situation might change in the future and if it does, we should know that we have other options as well.

The configuration of each supported Redis connector always has the following two steps:

1. Configuring the correct Maven dependency.
2. Configuring the correct Redis connection factory bean in the `redisConnectionFactory()` method of the `ApplicationContext` class.

Configuring the Jedis connector

Because Jedis is the default connector of Spring Data Redis, we don't have to make any changes to our pom.xml file. The only thing that we have to do is to add the Redis connection factory bean in our application context configuration. The correct Redis connection factory bean class for the Jedis connector is the JedisConnectionFactory class, and it has the following configuration properties:

Property	Description
dataBase	The index of the used database.
hostName	The hostname of the used Redis server.
password	The password used for authenticating with the Redis server.
poolConfig	The connection pool configuration that is given by using the redis.clients.jedis.JedisPoolConfig class.
port	The port of the used Redis server.
shardInfo	An alternative method for configuring the JedisConnectionFactory object. The configuration is given by using the redis.clients.jedis.JedisShardInfo class. This method has precedence over other colliding configuration properties.
timeout	The connection timeout.
usePool	A boolean value describing if connection pooling is used.

We will configure the Redis connection factory bean in the redisConnectionFactory() method of the ApplicationContext class. Our implementation includes the following steps:

1. Creating a new JedisConnectionFactory object.
2. Configuring the Redis connection factory bean.
3. Returning the created object.

The source code of the implemented redisConnectionFactory() method is given as follows:

```
@Bean
public RedisConnectionFactory redisConnectionFactory() {
  JedisConnectionFactory cf = new JedisConnectionFactory();

  cf.setHostName(env.getRequiredProperty("redis.host"));
  cf.setPort(Integer.parseInt(env.getRequiredProperty("redis.port")));

  return cf;
}
```

Configuring the JRedis connector

The first step is to configure the Maven dependencies of JRedis. We can configure the required dependencies by following these steps:

1. Exclude the transitive Jedis dependency from our build.
2. Add the forked JRedis connector as a dependency.

After we have followed the described steps, we should have the following dependency declarations in the `pom.xml` file:

```
<dependency>
    <groupId>org.springframework.data</groupId>
    <artifactId>spring-data-redis</artifactId>
    <version>1.0.1.RELEASE</version>
    <exclusions>
        <exclusion>
            <groupId>redis.clients</groupId>
            <artifactId>jedis</artifactId>
        </exclusion>
    </exclusions>
</dependency>
<dependency>
    <groupId>org.jredis</groupId>
    <artifactId>jredis-anthonylauzon</artifactId>
    <version>03122010</version>
</dependency>
```

The second step is to configure the used Redis connection factory bean. Because we want to use the JRedis connector, we have to use the `JRedisConnectionFactory` class. The configuration properties of this class are described in following table:

Property	Description
dataBase	The index of the used database.
hostName	The hostname of the used Redis server.
password	The password user for authenticating with the Redis server.
poolSize	The size of the connection pool.
port	The port of the used Redis server.
usePool	A `boolean` value describing if connection pooling is used.

In order to configure the Redis connector, we have to add the implementation of the `redisConnectionFactory()` method to the `ApplicationContext` class. We can do this by following these steps:

1. Create a new `JRedisConnectionFactory` object.
2. Configure the Redis connection factory bean.
3. Return the created object.

The source code of our Redis connection factory bean configuration is given as follows:

```
@Bean
public RedisConnectionFactory redisConnectionFactory() {
    JredisConnectionFactory cf = new JredisConnectionFactory();

    cf.setHostName(env.getRequiredProperty("redis.host"));
    cf.setPort(Integer.parseInt(env.getRequiredProperty("redis.
port")));

    return cf;
}
```

Configuring the RJC connector

First we have to configure the required Maven dependencies. This process includes the following steps:

1. Exclude the transitive Jedis dependency from our build.
2. Add the RJC connector as a dependency.

The dependency declarations, which we must add to the dependencies section of our `pom.xml` file, are given as follows:

```
<dependency>
    <groupId>org.springframework.data</groupId>
    <artifactId>spring-data-redis</artifactId>
    <version>1.0.1.RELEASE</version>
    <exclusions>
        <exclusion>
            <groupId>redis.clients</groupId>
            <artifactId>jedis</artifactId>
        </exclusion>
    </exclusions>
</dependency>
```

```
<dependency>
    <groupId>org.idevlab</groupId>
    <artifactId>rjc</artifactId>
    <version>0.7</version>
</dependency>
```

The last step is to add the configuration of the used Redis connection factory bean to our application context configuration class. Because we are using the RJC connector, the correct Redis connection factory class is `RjcConnectionFactory`. This class has the following configuration properties:

Property	Description
dataBase	The index of the used database.
hostName	The hostname of the used Redis server.
password	The password that used for authenticating with the Redis server.
port	The port of the used Redis server.
timeout	The value for connection timeout.
usePool	A `boolean` value describing if connection pooling is used.

Our implementation of the `redisConnectionFactory()` method includes the following steps:

1. Create a new `RjcConnectionFactory` object.
2. Configure the Redis connection factory bean.
3. Return the created object.

The source code of our Redis connection factory bean configuration is given as follows:

```
@Bean
public RedisConnectionFactory redisConnectionFactory() {
    RjcConnectionFactory cf = new RjcConnectionFactory();

    cf.setHostName(env.getRequiredProperty("redis.host"));
    cf.setPort(Integer.parseInt(env.getRequiredProperty("redis.
port")));

    return cf;
}
```

Configuring the SRP connector

The first step is to configure the Maven dependencies of the SRP Redis connector. We can configure the required dependencies by following these steps:

1. Exclude the transitive Jedis dependency from our build.
2. Add the SRP connector as a dependency.

This leads into the following dependency declarations:

```
<dependency>
    <groupId>org.springframework.data</groupId>
    <artifactId>spring-data-redis</artifactId>
    <version>1.0.1.RELEASE</version>
    <exclusions>
        <exclusion>
            <groupId>redis.clients</groupId>
            <artifactId>jedis</artifactId>
        </exclusion>
    </exclusions>
</dependency>
<dependency>
    <groupId>com.github.spullara.redis</groupId>
    <artifactId>client</artifactId>
    <version>0.2</version>
</dependency>
```

The second step is to configure the Redis connection factory bean. The correct connection factory bean class for the SRP connector is SrpConnectionFactory, and it has the following configuration properties:

Property	Description
hostName	The hostname of the used Redis server.
port	The port of the used Redis server.

We can configure the SRP connector by writing an implementation to the redisConnectionFactory() method. Our implementation has the following steps:

1. Create a new SrpConnectionFactory object.
2. Configure the Redis connection factory bean.
3. Return the created object.

The source code of our Redis connection factory bean configuration is given as follows:

```
@Bean
public RedisConnectionFactory redisConnectionFactory() {
    SrpConnectionFactory cf = new SrpConnectionFactory();

    cf.setHostName(env.getRequiredProperty("redis.host"));
    cf.setPort(Integer.parseInt(env.getRequiredProperty("redis.
port")));

    return cf;
}
```

Summary

In this chapter, we have learned that:

- Redis does not have complex dependencies, and it is easy to install Redis to a computer that runs a Unix-like operating system
- Some of the supported connectors do not support all features of Redis yet
- The configuration options that we can use when we are configuring our Redis connection depend on the used connector
- We should use the Jedis connector when we are writing applications by using Spring Data Redis

We have now learned how can set up a web application project that uses Spring Data Redis. In the next chapter, we will write some code and implement a contact manager application by using Spring Data Redis.

6
Building Applications with Spring Data Redis

We have learned how we can set up our project and configure the used Redis connection. Now it is time to expand our knowledge and learn how we can use Spring Data Redis in our applications. We will also prove that it is possible to use Redis as data storage of a web application.

> *Salvatore Sanfilippo* is a contributor of the Redis project and he has written a wonderful blog entry that describes how we can use Redis in our applications. This blog entry is available at http://antirez.com/post/take-advantage-of-redis-adding-it-to-your-stack.html.

In this chapter, we will cover:

- The basic design principles of a Redis data model
- The key components of Spring Data Redis
- How we can implement a CRUD application
- How we can use the publish/subscribe messaging pattern
- How we can use Spring Data Redis as an implementation of the cache abstraction provided by Spring Framework 3.1

Designing a Redis data model

The most important rules of designing a Redis data model are: Redis does not support ad hoc queries and it does not support relations in the same way than relational databases. Thus, designing a Redis data model is a total different ballgame than designing the data model of a relational database. The basic guidelines of a Redis data model design are given as follows:

- Instead of simply modeling the information stored in our data model, we have to also think how we want to search information from it. This often leads to a situation where we have to duplicate data in order to fulfill the requirements given to us. Don't be afraid to do this.

- We should not concentrate on normalizing our data model. Instead, we should combine the data that we need to handle as an unit into an aggregate.

- Since Redis does not support relations, we have to design and implement these relations by using the supported data structures. This means that we have to maintain these relations manually when they are changed. Because this might require a lot of effort and code, it could be wise to simply duplicate the information instead of using relations.

- It is always wise to spend a moment to verify that we are using the correct tool for the job.

 NoSQL Distilled, by *Martin Fowler* contains explanations of different NoSQL databases and their use cases, and can be found at `http://martinfowler.com/books/nosql.html`.

As we learned in *Chapter 1, Getting Started*, Redis supports multiple data structures. However, one question remained unanswered: which data structure should we use for our data? This question is addressed in the following table:

Data type	Description
String	A string is good choice for storing information that is already converted to a textual form. For instance, if we want to store HTML, JSON, or XML, a string should be our weapon of choice.
List	A list is a good choice if we will access it only near the start or end. This means that we should use it for representing queues or stacks.
Set	We should use a set if we need to get the size of a collection or check if a certain item belongs to it. Also, if we want to represent relations, a set is a good choice (for example, "who are John's friends?").
Sorted set	Sorted sets should be used in the same situations as sets when the ordering of items is important to us.
Hash	A hash is a perfect data structure for representing complex objects.

Key components

Spring Data Redis provides certain components that are the cornerstones of each application that uses it. This section provides a brief introduction to the components that we will later use to implement our example applications.

Atomic counters

Atomic counters are for Redis what sequences are for relational databases. Atomic counters guarantee that the value received by a client is unique. This makes these counters a perfect tool for creating unique IDs to our data that is stored in Redis. At the moment, Spring Data Redis offers two atomic counters: `RedisAtomicInteger` and `RedisAtomicLong`. These classes provide atomic counter operations for integers and longs.

RedisTemplate

The `RedisTemplate<K,V>` class is the central component of Spring Data Redis. It provides methods that we can use to communicate with a Redis instance. This class requires that two type parameters are given during its instantiation: the type of used Redis key and the type of the Redis value.

Operations

The `RedisTemplate` class provides two kinds of operations that we can use to store, fetch, and remove data from our Redis instance:

1. Operations that require that the key and the value are given every time an operation is performed. These operations are handy when we have to execute a single operation by using a key and a value.

2. Operations that are bound to a specific key that is given only once. We should use this approach when we have to perform multiple operations by using the same key.

The methods that require that a key and value is given every time an operation is performed are described in following list:

- `HashOperations<K,HK,HV> opsForHash()`: This method returns the operations that are performed on hashes

- `ListOperations<K,V> opsForList()`: This method returns the operations performed on lists

- `SetOperations<K,V> opsForSet()`: This method returns the operations performed on sets

- `ValueOperations<K,V> opsForValue()`: This method returns the operations performed on simple values

- `ZSetOperations<K,HK,HV> opsForZSet()`: This method returns the operations performed on sorted sets

The methods of the `RedisTemplate` class that allow us to execute multiple operations by using the same key are described in following list:

- `BoundHashOperarations<K,HK,HV> boundHashOps(K key)`: This method returns hash operations that are bound to the key given as a parameter

- `BoundListOperations<K,V> boundListOps(K key)`: This method returns list operations bound to the key given as a parameter

- `BoundSetOperations<K,V> boundSetOps(K key)`: This method returns set operations, which are bound to the given key

- `BoundValueOperations<K,V> boundValueOps(K key)`: This method returns operations performed to simple values that are bound to the given key

- `BoundZSetOperations<K,V> boundZSetOps(K key)`: This method returns operations performed on sorted sets that are bound to the key that is given as a parameter

The differences between these operations become clear to us when we start building our example applications.

Serializers

Because the data is stored in Redis as bytes, we need a method for converting our data to bytes and vice versa. Spring Data Redis provides an interface called `RedisSerializer<T>`, which is used in the serialization process. This interface has one type parameter that describes the type of the serialized object. Spring Data Redis provides several implementations of this interface. These implementations are described in the following table:

Serializer	Description
`GenericToStringSerializer<T>`	Serializes strings to bytes and vice versa. Uses the Spring `ConversionService` to transform objects to strings and vice versa.
`JacksonJsonRedisSerializer<T>`	Converts objects to JSON and vice versa.
`JdkSerializationRedisSerializer`	Provides Java based serialization to objects.
`OxmSerializer`	Uses the Object/XML mapping support of Spring Framework 3.
`StringRedisSerializer`	Converts strings to bytes and vice versa.

We can customize the serialization process of the RedisTemplate class by using the described serializers. The RedisTemplate class provides flexible configuration options that can be used to set the serializers that are used to serialize value keys, values, hash keys, hash values, and string values.

The default serializer of the RedisTemplate class is JdkSerializationRedisSerializer. However, the string serializer is an exception to this rule. StringRedisSerializer is the serializer that is by default used to serialize string values.

Implementing a CRUD application

This section describes two different ways for implementing a CRUD application that is used to manage contact information. First, we will learn how we can implement a CRUD application by using the default serializer of the RedisTemplate class. Second, we will learn how we can use value serializers and implement a CRUD application that stores our data in JSON format.

Both of these applications will also share the same domain model. This domain model consists of two classes: Contact and Address. The information content of these classes has already been described in *Chapter 2, Getting Started with Spring Data JPA*. However, we have made the following changes to these classes:

* We removed the JPA specific annotations from them
* We use these classes in our web layer as form objects and they no longer have any other methods than getters and setters

The domain model is not the only thing that is shared by these examples. They also share the interface that declares the service methods for the Contact class. The source code of the ContactService interface is given as follows:

```
public interface ContactService {
    public Contact add(Contact added);
    public Contact deleteById(Long id) throws NotFoundException;
    public List<Contact> findAll();
    public Contact findById(Long id) throws NotFoundException;
    public Contact update(Contact updated) throws NotFoundException;
}
```

Both of these applications will communicate with the used Redis instance by using the Jedis connector that was described in *Chapter 5, Getting Started with Spring Data Redis*.

Regardless of the user's approach, we can implement a CRUD application with Spring Data Redis by following these steps:

1. Configure the application context.
2. Implement the CRUD functions.

Let's get started and find out how we can implement the CRUD functions for contact information.

Using default serializers

This subsection describes how we can implement a CRUD application by using the default serializers of the RedisTemplate class. This means that StringRedisSerializer is used to serialize string values, and JdkSerializationRedisSerializer serializes other objects.

Configuring the application context

We can configure the application context of our application by making the following changes to the ApplicationContext class:

1. Configuring the Redis template bean.
2. Configuring the Redis atomic long bean.

Configuring the Redis template bean

We can configure the Redis template bean by adding a redisTemplate() method to the ApplicationContext class and annotating this method with the @Bean annotation. We can implement this method by following these steps:

1. Create a new RedisTemplate object.
2. Set the used connection factory to the created RedisTemplate object.
3. Return the created object.

The source code of the redisTemplate() method is given as follows:

```
@Bean
public RedisTemplate redisTemplate() {
  RedisTemplate<String, String> redis = new RedisTemplate<String,
String>();

  redis.setConnectionFactory(redisConnectionFactory());

  return redis;
}
```

Configuring the Redis atomic long bean

We start the configuration of the Redis atomic long bean by adding a method called `redisAtomicLong()` to the `ApplicationContext` class and annotating the method with the `@Bean` annotation. Our next task is to implement this method by following these steps:

1. Create a new `RedisAtomicLong` object. Pass the name of the used Redis counter and the Redis connection factory as constructor parameters.

2. Return the created object.

The source code of the `redisAtomicLong()` method is given as follows:

```
@Bean
public RedisAtomicLong redisAtomicLong() {
    return new RedisAtomicLong("contact", redisConnectionFactory());
}
```

 If we need to create IDs for instances of different classes, we can use the same Redis counter. Thus, we have to configure only one Redis atomic long bean.

CRUD

Before we can start implementing the CRUD functions for the `Contact` class, we have to discuss a bit about the Redis data model of our application. We use two different data types for storing contact information to Redis. The information of a single contact is stored in a hash because as we know, a hash is a great structure for storing the information of complex objects. Also, we store the key of each contact in a set because a set provides us a fast capability to check if a contact exists. We also use this set when we are fetching a list of all contacts from Redis.

Our next step is to implement the `ContactService` interface that declares CRUD operations for contacts. Let's start by creating a dummy service implementation and add the actual CRUD methods later. The implementation of this class includes the following steps:

1. Implementing the `ContactService` interface.

2. Annotating the created class with the `@Service` annotation.

3. Adding the required dependencies as private members of the created class and annotating these members with the `@Resource` annotation. We need to have a reference to both the `RedisTemplate` and `RedisAtomicLong` objects.

The source code of our dummy implementation is given as follows:

```
@Service
public class RedisContactService implements ContactService {

    @Resource
    private RedisAtomicLong contactIdCounter;

    @Resource
    private RedisTemplate<String, String> redisTemplate;

    //Add methods here.
}
```

The next step is to implement common methods that are used by the methods declared by the `ContactService` interface. These private methods are described in the following table:

Method	Description
`String buildKey(Long contactId)`	Returns a key for a contact.
`Contact buildContact(String key)`	Fetches the information of a contact and returns the found contact.
`Contact buildContact(Long id)`	Fetches the information of a contact and returns the found contact.
`boolean contactDoesNotExist(Long id)`	Returns false if a contact is found with the given ID and true otherwise.
`String persist(Contact persisted)`	Saves the contact information and returns the key of the contact.

First, we have to implement the method that is used to build keys for our contacts. Our implementation of the `buildKey()` method is quite simple. We build the key by appending the contact ID given as a parameter to a string `contact` and returning the resulting string. The source code of the `buildKey()` method is given as follows:

```
private String buildKey(Long contactId) {
    return "contact" + contactId;
}
```

Second, we have to implement the method that is used to fetch contact information by using the key of the contact. We can implement the `buildContact(String key)` method by following these steps:

1. Create a new `Contact` object.
2. Fetch the information of the contact from the hash.

 We use bound hash operations because this way we have to provide the key only once.

3. Return the created object.

The source code of the implemented method is given as follows:

```
private Contact buildContact(String key) {
    Contact contact = new Contact();

    BoundHashops ops = redisTemplate.boundHashOps(key);

    contact.setId((Long) ops.get("id"));
    contact.setEmailAddress((String) ops.get("emailAddress"));
    contact.setFirstName((String) ops.get("firstName"));
    contact.setLastName((String) ops.get("lastName"));
    contact.setPhoneNumber((String) ops.get("phoneNumber"));

    Address address = new Address();
    address.setStreetAddress((String) ops.get("streetAddress"));
    address.setPostCode((String) ops.get("postCode"));
    address.setPostOffice((String) ops.get("postOffice"));
    address.setState((String) ops.get("state"));
    address.setCountry((String) ops.get("country"));
    contact.setAddress(address);

    return contact;
}
```

Third, we have to implement the method that fetches contact information by using the ID of the contact. Our implementation of the `buildContact(Long id)` method is rather simple, and it includes the following steps:

1. Build the key of the contact.
2. Get the contact by using the created key.
3. Return the found contact.

The source code of this method is given as follows:

```
private Contact buildContact(Long id) {
    String key = buildKey(id);
    return buildContact(key);
}
```

Fourth, we have to implement the method used to verify whether a contact in question exists or not. Our implementation of the contactDoesNotExist() method consists of the following steps:

1. Create the key of the contact.
2. Check if the key is found from the contacts set by calling the isMember() method of the SetOperations class, and passing the name of the set and the key as parameters.

 We use setOperations because we execute only one command.

3. Inverse the return value of the isMember() method and return the inverted value.

The source code of this method is given as follows:

```
private boolean contactDoesNotExist(Long id) {
    String key = buildKey(id);
    return !redisTemplate.opsForSet().isMember("contacts", key);
}
```

Fifth, we have to implement the method that saves the information of a single contact. Our implementation of the persist() method includes the following steps:

1. If the persisted Contact object does not have an ID, create one calling the incrementAndGet() method of the RedisAtomicLong class and set the received Long object as the contact ID.
2. Build a key for the persisted contact.
3. Save the contact in the hash.
4. Return the persisted contact.

The source code of the `persist()` method is given as follows:

```java
private String persist(Contact persisted) {
    Long id = persisted.getId();
    if (id == null) {
        id = contactIdCounter.incrementAndGet();
        persisted.setId(id);
    }

    String contactKey = buildKey(id);

    BoundHashops ops = redisTemplate.boundHashOps(contactKey);

    ops.put("id", persisted.getId());
    ops.put("emailAddress", persisted.getEmailAddress());
    ops.put("firstName", persisted.getFirstName());
    ops.put("lastName", persisted.getLastName());
    ops.put("phoneNumber", persisted.getPhoneNumber());

    Address address = persisted.getAddress();

    ops.put("streetAddress", address.getStreetAddress());
    ops.put("postCode", address.getPostCode());
    ops.put("postOffice", address.getPostOffice());
    ops.put("state", address.getState());
    ops.put("country", address.getCountry());

    return contactKey;
}
```

We have now implemented the common methods of the `RedisContactService` class. Let's move on and find out how we can provide the CRUD operations for the contact information.

Create

We can create a new contact by following these steps:

1. Save the added contact to the hash.
2. Add the key of the contact to our contact set.
3. Return the added contact.

The source code of the `add()` method is given as follows:

```
@Override
public Contact add(Contact added) {
  String key = persist(added);
  redisTemplate.opsForSet().add("contacts", key);
  return added;
}
```

Read

We have to provide two methods that are used to fetch contact information from Redis. The first method is used to return a list of existing contacts and the second one is used to find the information of a single contact.

First, we have to implement a method that is used to return a list of existing contacts. We can implement the `findAll()` method by following these steps:

1. Create a new `ArrayList` object that is used to store the found `Contact` objects.

2. Get the keys of existing contacts from the contact set.

3. Get the information of each existing contact from the hash and add them to the created `ArrayList` object.

4. Return the list of contacts.

The source code of the implemented method is given as follows:

```
@Override
public List<Contact> findAll() {
  List<Contact> contacts = new ArrayList<Contact>();

  Collection<String> keys = redisTemplate.opsForSet().
members("contacts");

  for (String key: keys) {
    Contact contact = buildContact(key);
    contacts.add(contact);
  }

  return contacts;
}
```

Second, we have to implement a method that is used to return the information of a single contact. We can implement the `findById()` method by following these steps:

1. Check that the contact exists. If contact does not exist, throw `NotFoundException`.

2. Get the contact from the hash.

3. Return the found contact.

The source code of our method is given as follows:

```
@Override
public Contact findById(Long id) throws NotFoundException {
  if (contactDoesNotExist(id)) {
    throw new NotFoundException("No contact found with id: " + id);
    }
  return buildContact(id);
}
```

Update

We can update the information of an existing contact by following these steps:

1. Check if that contact exists. If no contact is found, throw a `NotFoundException`.

2. Save the updated contact information in the hash.

3. Return the updated contact.

The source code of the `update()` method is given as follows:

```
@Override
public Contact update(Contact updated) throws NotFoundException {
  if (contactDoesNotExist(updated.getId())) {
    throw new NotFoundException("No contact found with id: " +
updated.getId());
  }
  persist(updated);
  return updated;
}
```

Delete

We can delete the information of a contact by following these steps:

1. Get a reference of the deleted contact.

 We use the findById() method because it throws NotFoundException if the contact is not found.

2. Build a key of the deleted contact.
3. Remove the contact from our contact set.
4. Remove the information of a contact from the hash.
5. Return the deleted contact.

The source code of the deleteById() method is given as follows:

```java
@Override
public Contact deleteById(Long id) throws NotFoundException {
  Contact deleted = findById(id);
  String key = buildKey(id);

  redisTemplate.opsForSet().remove("contacts", key);

  BoundHashOperations operations = redisTemplate.boundHashOps(key);

  operations.delete("id");
  operations.delete("emailAddress");
  operations.delete("firstName");
  operations.delete("lastName");
  operations.delete("phoneNumber");

  operations.delete("streetAddress");
  operations.delete("postCode");
  operations.delete("postOffice");
  operations.delete("state");
  operations.delete("country");

  return deleted;
}
```

Storing data in JSON

If we store object information in a hash, we have to write a lot of boilerplate code that is used to save, read, and delete contact information. This subsection describes how we reduce the amount of required code and implement a CRUD application that stores the contact information in JSON format. This means that `StringRedisSerializer` is used to serialize string values and that `JacksonJsonRedisSerializer` transforms our `Contact` objects into JSON.

Configuring the application context

We can configure the application context of our application by following these steps:

1. Configure the value serializer bean.
2. Configure the Redis template.
3. Configure the Redis atomic long bean.

Configuring the value serializer bean

We can configure the value serializer bean by adding a `contactSerializer()` method to the `ApplicationContext` class and annotating it with the `@Bean` annotation. We can implement this method by following these steps:

1. Create a new `JacksonJsonRedisSerializer` object and pass the type of the `Contact` class as a constructor parameter.
2. Return the created object.

The source code of the `contactSerializer()` method is given as follows:

```
@Bean
public RedisSerializer<Contact> valueSerializer() {
    return new JacksonJsonRedisSerializer<Contact>(Contact.class);
}
```

Configuring the Redis template bean

We can configure the Redis template by adding a `redisTemplate()` method to the `ApplicationContext` class, annotating it with the `@Bean` annotation and configuring the Redis template in its implementation. We can implement this method by following these steps:

1. Create a new `RedisTemplate` object and give the type of our key and value as type parameters.
2. Set the used connection factory.

3. Set the used value serializer.

4. Return the created object.

The source code of the `redisTemplate()` method is given as follows:

```
@Bean
public RedisTemplate redisTemplate() {
    RedisTemplate<String, Contact> redisTemplate = new
RedisTemplate<String, Contact>();
    redisTemplate.setConnectionFactory(redisConnectionFactory());
    redisTemplate.setValueSerializer(valueSerializer());

    return redisTemplate;
}
```

Configuring the Redis atomic long bean

We will start the configuration of the Redis atomic long bean by adding a `redisAtomicLong()` method to the `ApplicationContext` class and annotating it with the `@Bean` annotation. Our next step is to implement this method by following these steps:

1. Create a new `RedisAtomicLong` object. Pass the name of the used Redis counter and the Redis connection factory as constructor parameters.

2. Return the created object.

The source code of the `redisAtomicLong()` method is given as follows:

```
@Bean
public RedisAtomicLong redisAtomicLong() {
    return new RedisAtomicLong("contact", redisConnectionFactory());
}
```

CRUD

First we have to talk about our Redis data model. We store the contact information to Redis, using two different data types. We store the information of a single contact to Redis as a string value. This makes sense since the contact information is transformed to the JSON format before it is saved. We will also use a set that contains the JSON representations of the `Contact` objects. We have to duplicate the information because otherwise we would not be able to show a list of contacts.

We can provide the CRUD operations for the `Contact` objects by implementing the `ContactService` interface. Let's start by creating a dummy service implementation and adding or implementing the actual CRUD operations later. The steps needed to create a dummy service implementation are described as follows:

1. Implement the `ContactService` interface.
2. Annotate the created class with the `@Service` annotation.
3. Add the required dependencies as private members of the created class and annotate these members with the `@Resource` annotation. We need to have a reference to both the `RedisTemplate` and `RedisAtomicLong` objects.

The source code of our dummy service implementation is given as follows:

```
@Service
public class RedisContactService implements ContactService {

    @Resource
    private RedisAtomicLong contactIdCounter;

    @Resource
    private RedisTemplate<String, Contact> redisTemplate;

    //Add methods here
}
```

We also have to implement some utility methods that are used by the methods declared by the `ContactService` interface. These private methods are described in the following table:

Method	Description
`String buildKey(Long contactId)`	Returns a key for a contact.
`void persist(Contact persisted)`	Saves the contact information to a string value.

First, we have to implement a method that is used to build keys for the persisted `Contact` objects. The implementation of the `buildKey()` method is simple. We build the key by appending the contact ID given as a parameter to a string `contact` and return the resulting string. The source code of the `buildKey()` method is given as follows:

```
private String buildKey(Long contactId) {
    return "contact" + contactId;
}
```

Second, we have to implement a `persist()` method that saves the contact information. We can do this by performing the following steps:

1. If the contact ID is null, get a new ID and set the received `Long` object as an ID of the `Contact` object.

2. Create a key for the contact.

3. Save the contact information as a string value.

 We use value operations because we need to execute only one operation.

The source code of the `persist()` method is given as follows:

```
private void persist(Contact persisted) {
  Long id = persisted.getId();
  if (id == null) {
      id = contactIdCounter.incrementAndGet();
      persisted.setId(id);
    }
  String key = buildKey(persisted.getId());
  redisTemplate.opsForValue().set(key, persisted);
}
```

We are now ready to start implementing the CRUD operations for contacts. Let's move on and find out how it is done.

Create

We can implement a method that adds new contacts by following these steps:

1. Save the added contact.

2. Add the contact information into the contact set.

3. Return the added contact.

The source code of the `add()` method is given as follows:

```
@Override
public Contact add(Contact added) {
    persist(added);
    redisTemplate.opsForSet().add("contacts", added);
    return added;
}
```

Read

Our application has two views that present contact information: the first one shows a list of contacts and the second one shows the information of a single contact.

First, we have to implement a method that fetches all the contacts from Redis. We can implement the findAll() method by following these steps:

1. Fetch all the contacts from the contact set.
2. Create a new ArrayList object and return the created object.

The source code of the findAll() method is given as follows:

```
@Override
public List<Contact> findAll() {
    Collection<Contact> contacts = redisTemplate.opsForSet().
members("contacts");
    return new ArrayList<Contact>(contacts);
}
```

Second, we have to implement a method that returns the information of a single contact. Our implementation of the findById() method includes the following steps:

1. Create the key of the contact.
2. Get the Contact object from Redis.
3. If no contact is found, throw NotFoundException.
4. Return the found object.

The source code of the findById() method is given as follows:

```
@Override
public Contact findById(Long id) throws NotFoundException {
    String key = buildKey(id);
    Contact found = redisTemplate.opsForValue().get(key);

    if (found == null) {
        throw new NotFoundException("No contact found with id: {}" +
id);
    }

    return found;
}
```

Update

We can update the information of an existing contact by following these steps:

1. Get the old contact information from Redis.

2. Save the updated contact information.

3. Remove the old contact information from the contact set. This ensures that our set does not contain duplicate entries for the same contact.

4. Add the updated contact information to the contact set.

5. Return the updated contact.

The source code of the update() method is given as follows:

```
@Override
public Contact update(Contact updated) throws NotFoundException {
    Contact old = findById(updated.getId());

    persist(updated);
    redisTemplate.opsForSet().remove("contacts", old);
    redisTemplate.opsForSet().add("contacts", updated);

    return updated;
}
```

Delete

We can delete contact information by following these steps:

1. Find the deleted contact by calling the findById() method. This ensures that NotFoundException is thrown if the contact is not found.

2. Build a key used to get the contact information.

3. Remove the deleted contact from the contact set.

4. Remove the JSON representation of the deleted contact.

5. Return the deleted contact.

The source code of the delete() method is given as follows:

```
@Override
public Contact deleteById(Long id) throws NotFoundException {
    Contact deleted = findById(id);

    String key = buildKey(id);
```

```
redisTemplate.opsForSet().remove("contacts", deleted);
redisTemplate.opsForValue().set(key, null);

return deleted;
}
```

The publish/subscribe messaging pattern

Redis also includes an implementation of the publish/subscribe messaging pattern. This section demonstrates how we can use Spring Data Redis for the purpose of sending and receiving messages. As an example, we will modify the CRUD application that stores the contact information as JSON to send notifications when a new contact is added, contact information is updated, and a contact is deleted.

We can implement this requirement by performing the following steps:

1. Create message listeners that process the received messages.
2. Configure the application context of our application.
3. Send messages by using the RedisTemplate class.

This section also describes how we can ensure that our implementation is working correctly.

Creating message listeners

There are two ways to create message listeners by using Spring Data Redis: we can implement the MessageListener interface or we can create a POJO message listener and use the MessageListenerAdapter class to delegate messages to it. Both of these approaches are discussed in this subsection.

Implementing the MessageListener interface

The first way to create a message listener is to implement the MessageListener interface. Our implementation includes the following steps:

1. Create a new Logger object that is used to log the received messages.
2. Create a new StringRedisSerializer object that is used to transform byte arrays to String objects.
3. Implement the onMessage() method declared by the MessageListener interface. This method simply logs the received message.

The source code of the ContactListener class is given as follows:

```
public class ContactMessageListener implements MessageListener {

    private final static Logger LOGGER = LoggerFactory.getLogger(Conta
ctMessageListener.class);

    private RedisSerializer<String> stringSerializer = new
StringRedisSerializer();

    @Override
    public void onMessage(Message message, byte[] pattern) {
        LOGGER.debug("MessageListener - received message: {} on
channel: {}", stringSerializer.deserialize(message.getBody()),
stringSerializer.deserialize(message.getChannel()));
    }
}
```

Creating a POJO message listener

The second way to create message listeners is to create a normal Java class. We can do this by following these steps:

1. Create a new Logger object that is used to log the received messages.
2. Create a message handler method called handleMessage() that takes the Contact object and a String object as parameters.
3. Implement the handleMessage() method. This method logs the received message.

The source code of the ContactPOJOMessageListener class is given as follows:

```
public class ContactPOJOMessageListener {

    private static final Logger LOGGER = LoggerFactory.getLogger(Conta
ctPOJOMessageListener.class);

    public void handleMessage(Contact contact, String channel) {
        LOGGER.debug("Received contact: {} on channel: {}", contact,
channel);
    }
}
```

Configuring the application context

We have to make the following changes to the application context configuration:

1. Configure the message listener beans.
2. Configure a message listener adapter bean.
3. Configure a message listener container bean.

Configuring the message listener beans

First, we have to configure our message listener beans. The configuration is rather simple. We just create new message listener objects and return the created objects. The source code of the message listener bean configuration is given as follows:

```
@Bean
public ContactMessageListener contactMessageListener() {
    return new ContactMessageListener();
}

@Bean
public ContactPOJOMessageListener contactPOJOMessageListener() {
    return new ContactPOJOMessageListener();
}
```

Configuring the message listener adapter bean

Next we have to configure the message listener adapter bean that is used to delegate the messages forward to our POJO message listener. We can configure this bean by following these steps:

1. Create a new `MessageListenerAdapter` object and pass the `ContactPOJOMessageListener` object as a constructor parameter.
2. Set the serializer that is used to transform the received message to a `Contact` object.
3. Return the created object.

The source code of the `messageListenerAdapter()` method is given as follows:

```
@Bean
public MessageListenerAdapter messageListenerAdapter() {
    MessageListenerAdapter adapter = new MessageListenerAdapter(contac
tPOJOMessageListener());
    adapter.setSerializer(contactSerializer());
    return adapter;
}
```

The defaultListenerMethod property of the MessageListenerAdapter class is used to configure the name of the message handler method. The default value of this property is handleMessage.

Configuring the message listener container bean

The **message listener container** is a component that listens to the messages that are sent through the different channels and forwards these messages to the registered message listeners. We can configure this component by following these steps:

1. Create a new RedisMessageListenerContainer object.

2. Set the used Redis connection factory.

3. Register the message listeners and specify the subscribed channels.

4. Return the created object.

The source code of our configuration is given as follows:

```
@Bean
public RedisMessageListenerContainer redisMessageListenerContainer() {
    RedisMessageListenerContainer container = new
RedisMessageListenerContainer();

    container.setConnectionFactory(redisConnectionFactory());
    container.addMessageListener(messageListenerAdapter(),
    Arrays.asList(
            new ChannelTopic("newContacts"),
            new ChannelTopic("updatedContacts"),
            new ChannelTopic("removedContacts")
    ));
    container.addMessageListener(contactMessageListener(),
    Arrays.asList(
            new ChannelTopic("newContacts"),
            new ChannelTopic("updatedContacts"),
            new ChannelTopic("removedContacts")
    ));

    return container;
}
```

Sending messages with RedisTemplate

We can send publish messages to different channels by using the
`convertAndSend(String channel, Object message)` method of the
`RedisTemplate` class. This subsection describes how we can send notifications
about new contacts, updated contacts, and removed contacts by using this method.

Create

In order to send change notifications about new contacts, we have to modify the
`add()` method of the `RedisContactService` class to call the `convertAndSend()`
method of the `RedisTemplate` class after the information of a new contact is saved
successfully. The source code of our new `add()` method is given as follows:

```
@Override
public Contact add(Contact added) {
    persist(added);
    redisTemplate.opsForSet().add("contacts", added);
    redisTemplate.convertAndSend("newContacts", added);

    return added;
}
```

Update

We can send notifications about updated contacts by modifying the `update()`
method of the `RedisContactService` class. We simply call the `convertAndSend()`
method of the `RedisTemplate` class after the contact information is updated. The
source code of the new `update()` method is given as follows:

```
@Override
public Contact update(Contact updated) throws NotFoundException {
    Contact old = findById(updated.getId());

    persist(updated);
    redisTemplate.opsForSet().remove("contacts", old);
    redisTemplate.opsForSet().add("contacts", updated);
    redisTemplate.convertAndSend("updatedContacts", updated);

    return updated;
}
```

Delete

We can send a notification about the deleted contacts by making a small change in the deleteById() method of the RedisContactService class. After the contact information is deleted, we will call the convertAndSend() method of the RedisTemplate class, which sends the notification message. The source code of the modified deleteById() method is given as follows:

```
@Override
public Contact deleteById(Long id) throws NotFoundException {
    Contact deleted = findById(id);

    String key = buildKey(id);

    redisTemplate.opsForSet().remove("contacts", deleted);
    redisTemplate.opsForValue().set(key, null);
    redisTemplate.convertAndSend("removedContacts", deleted);

    return deleted;
}
```

Verifying the wanted behaviour

We have now implemented our message listeners and modified our application to send a notification message every time the contact information is changed. Our next step is to verify that our implementation is working as expected.

We can confirm this by making changes to the contact information and making sure that log lines written by our message listeners appear in the application's log. The loglines that are written when a new contact is added are given as follows:

```
DEBUG - ContactMessageListener     - Received message: {"id":9,"add
ress":{"country":"","streetAddress":"","postCode":"","postOffice":"
","state":""},"emailAddress":"","firstName":"Foo","lastName":"Bar"-
,"phoneNumber":""} on channel: newContacts
DEBUG - ContactPOJOMessageListener - Received contact: com.packtpub.
springdata.redis.model.Contact@543d8ee8[id=9,address=com.packtpub.
springdata.redis.model.Address@15714c8d[country=,streetAddress=,postCo
de=,postOffice=,state=],emailAddress=,firstName=Foo,lastName=Bar,phone
Number=] on channel: null
```

 Note that the channel information passed to a POJO message handler is always null. This is a known bug of Spring Data Redis. More information about this is available at https://jira.springsource.org/browse/DATAREDIS-98.

Using Spring cache abstraction with Spring Data Redis

The cache abstraction of Spring Framework 3.1 applies caching to Java methods. When a cached method is called, the cache abstraction will check from the cache if the method has been called earlier by using the same parameters. If this is the case, then the return value is fetched from the cache and the method is not executed. Otherwise, the method is executed and its return value is stored in the cache.

 The cache abstraction of Spring Framework 3.1 is explained in more detail at http://static.springsource.org/spring/docs/3.1.x/spring-framework-reference/html/cache.html.

Spring Data Redis provides an implementation of the Spring cache abstraction. Using Redis as a cache has two benefits over using local caching implementations such as Ehcache:

- It can be used as a centralized cache that is shared by each servlet container or application server that runs our application. This reduces the overall number of database queries, which reduces the load of our database server and increases the performance of all the servers.

- The cache will not be emptied until we empty it. This means that we can restart our servlet container or application server without losing the information stored in the cache. After our server is restarted, it can take full advantage of the cached information right away. There is no need to warm up the cache.

This section describes how we can use Spring Data Redis for the purpose of adding a caching support to an application that uses the JPA Criteria API. This application has been originally introduced in *Chapter 3, Building Queries with Spring Data JPA*. The requirements of our caching example are as follows:

- The method calls to the method that finds the information of a single contact from the database must be cached

- When the information of a contact is updated, the information stored in the cache must be updated as well

- When a contact is deleted, the deleted contact must be removed from the cache

We can add caching support to our example application by following these steps:

1. Configure the Spring cache abstraction.
2. Identify the cached methods.

We will also learn how we can verify that the Spring cache abstraction is working correctly.

Configuring the Spring cache abstraction

We can configure the Spring cache abstraction by making the following changes to the application context configuration of our application:

1. Enable the caching annotations.
2. Configure the host and port of the used Redis instance in the used properties file.
3. Configure the Redis connection factory bean.
4. Configure the Redis template bean.
5. Configure the cache manager bean.

Enabling caching annotations

We can enable the caching annotations by annotating our application context configuration class with the `@EnableCaching` annotation. The relevant part of the `ApplicationContext` class is given as follows:

```
@Configuration
@ComponentScan(basePackages = {
        "com.packtpub.springdata.jpa.controller",
        "com.packtpub.springdata.jpa.service"
})
@EnableCaching
@EnableTransactionManagement
@EnableWebMvc
@EnableJpaRepositories("com.packtpub.springdata.jpa.repository")
@PropertySource("classpath:application.properties")
public class ApplicationContext extends WebMvcConfigurerAdapter {

    @Resource
    private Environment env;

    //Bean declarations
}
```

Configuring the host and port of the used Redis instance

In order to configure the host and port of the used Redis instance, we have to add the following lines to the `application.properties` file:

```
redis.host = localhost
redis.port = 6379
```

Configuring the Redis connection factory bean

We can configure the Redis connection factory bean by adding a `redisConnectionFactory()` method to the `ApplicationContext` class and annotating this method with the `@Bean` annotation. We can implement this method by following these steps:

1. Create a new `JedisConnectionFactory` object.
2. Configure the host and port of the used Redis instance.
3. Return the created object.

The source code of the `redisConnectionFactory()` method is given as follows:

```
@Bean
public RedisConnectionFactory redisConnectionFactory() {
    JedisConnectionFactory cf = new JedisConnectionFactory();

    cf.setHostName(env.getRequiredProperty("redis.host"));
    cf.setPort(Integer.parseInt(env.getRequiredProperty("redis.
port")));

    return cf;
}
```

Configuring the Redis template bean

In order to configure the Redis template bean, we have to add a `redisTemplate()` method to the `ApplicationContext` class and annotate this method with the `@Bean` annotation. Our implementation of this method includes the following steps:

1. Create a new `RedisTemplate` object.
2. Set the used Redis connection factory.
3. Return the created object.

The source code of the `redisTemplate()` method is given as follows:

```
@Bean
public RedisTemplate redisTemplate() {
    RedisTemplate<String, String> redisTemplate = new
RedisTemplate<String, String>();
    redisTemplate.setConnectionFactory(redisConnectionFactory());

    return redisTemplate;
}
```

Configuring the cache manager bean

Our last step is to configure the cache manager bean. We can do this by adding the `cacheManager()` method to the `ApplicationContext` class and annotating this method with the `@Bean` annotation. We can implement this method by following these steps:

1. Create a new `RedisCacheManager` object and provide the used Redis template as a constructor parameter.

2. Return the created object.

The source code of the `cacheManager()` method is given as follows:

```
@Bean
public RedisCacheManager cacheManager() {
    return new RedisCacheManager(redisTemplate());
}
```

Identifying the cached methods

We have now configured the Spring cache abstraction and we are ready to identify the cached methods. This subsection describes how we can add contact information in the cache, update contact information that is already stored in the cache, and delete the contact information from the cache.

Adding contact information to the cache

In order to add contact information to the cache, we must cache the method calls to the findById() method of the RepositoryContactService class. We can do this by annotating the method with the @Cacheable annotation and providing the name of the cache. This tells the cache abstraction that the returned contact should be added to the contacts cache by using the provided ID as a key. The source code of the findById() method is given as follows:

```
@Cacheable("contacts")
@Transactional(readOnly = true)
@Override
public Contact findById(Long id) throws NotFoundException {
    //Implementation remains unchanged.
}
```

Updating the contact information to the cache

We can update the contact information that is stored in the cache by annotating the update() method of the RepositoryContactService class with the @CachePut annotation. We will also have to provide the name of the cache and specify that the id property of the ContactDTO object is used as a key when the return value of this method is updated to the cache. The source code of the update() method is given as follows:

```
@CachePut(value = "contacts", key="#p0.id")
@Transactional(rollbackFor = NotFoundException.class)
@Override
public Contact update(ContactDTO updated) throws NotFoundException {
    //Implementation remains unchanged.
}
```

Deleting contact information from the cache

We can delete contact information from the cache by annotating the deleteById() method with the @CacheEvict annotation and providing the name of the cache as its value. This means that the cache abstraction removes the deleted contact from the cache after the method has been executed. The removed contact is identified by the ID given as a method parameter. The source code of the deleteById() method is given as follows:

```
@CacheEvict("contacts")
@Transactional(rollbackFor = NotFoundException.class)
@Override
public Contact deleteById(Long id) throws NotFoundException {
  //Implementation remains unchanged
}
```

Verifying that the Spring cache abstraction is working

We have now successfully added caching to our example application. We can verify that the Spring cache abstraction is working properly by using the cached methods and looking for the following lines from the log file of our application:

```
DEBUG - RedisConnectionUtils        - Opening Redis Connection
DEBUG - RedisConnectionUtils        - Closing Redis Connection
```

If these lines are found from the log file it can mean that:

- The contact information is fetched from the cache instead of the used database
- The contact information is updated to the cache
- The contact information is removed from the cache

Summary

In this chapter, we have learned that:

- Designing a Redis data model is totally different from designing a data model of a relational database
- We can use Redis as data storage of a web application
- Spring Data Redis provides a clean integration with the Redis publish/ subscribe implementation
- We can use Redis as a centralized cache of our application by using the Spring cache abstraction

Index

Symbols

@Bean annotation 117
@CachePut annotation 133
 @ComponentScan annotation 94
@ComponentScan annotation 20
@Configuration annotation 20, 94
@EnableCaching annotation 130
@EnableJpaRepositories annotation 20
@EnableTransactionManagement
       annotation 20
@EnableWebMcv annotation 20
@EnableWebMvc annotation 94
@MappedSuperclass annotation 30
@NamedNativeQueries annotation 47
@NamedQueries annotation 47
@Param annotation 48, 50
@PersistenceContext annotation 31
@PropertySource annotation 20
@Query annotation
  about 49
  cons 51
  pros 51
  query method, creating 50
  service method, creating 51
@Repository annotation 34
@Resource annotation 37
@Service annotation 37
@SqlResultSetMapping annotation 47, 50
@Transactional annotation 37

A

add() method 114
Address class
  about 28

addresses, creating 28, 29
address information, updating 30
Address objects
  creating 28, 29
AOF, persistence mechanisms
  about 14
  advantage 14
Append Only File. *See* AOF, persistence
       mechanism
ApplicationContext class 21
application context configuration
  loading 23, 24
application context configuration class
  application context configuration skeleton,
       creating 20
  creating 20
  data source bean, configuring 21
  entity manager factory bean,
       configuring 22
  transaction manager bean, configuring 23
application context configuration skeleton
  creating 20, 21
application context, publish/subscribe
       messaging pattern
  configuring 125
  message listener adapter bean,
       configuring 125
  message listener beans, configuring 125
  message listener container bean,
       configuring 126
Atomic counters
  about 105
  RedisAtomicInteger 105
  RedisAtomicLong 105

B

BaseEntity class 31
BaseRepositoryFactoryBean class 88
BaseRepositoryImpl class 32
base repository interface
  creating 84
  implementing 85
BoneCP 17
boolean contactDoesNotExist(Long id)
        method 110
BoundHashOperarations<K,HK,HV>
        boundHashOps(K key) method 106
BoundListOperations<K,V>
        boundListOps(K key) method 106
BoundSetOperations<K,V> boundSetOps(K
        key) method 106
BoundZSetOperations<K,V>
        boundZSetOps(K key) method 106
buildContact(Long id) method 111
buildContact(String key) method 111
buildKey() method 110
build() method 26
buildPageSpecification() method 69, 81, 82

C

cached methods, Spring cache abstraction
  identifying 132
cacheManager() method 132
channel 15
code generation Maven plugin
  configuring 56
components, Spring Data JPA
  Database 18
  data source 17
  JPA provider 17
  Spring Framework 18
configuration properties,
        JedisConnectionFactory class
  dataBase 97
  hostName 97
  password 97
  poolConfig 97
  port 97
  shardInfo 97
  timeout 97
  usePool 97

connectors, Spring Data Redis
  Jedis 95
  JRedis 95
  RJC 96
  SRP 96
cons, JPA Criteria API 55
cons, named query 49
cons, @Query annotation 51
cons, Querydsl 59
cons, query generation from method
        name 46
Contact buildContact(Long id) method 110
Contact buildContact(String key)
        method 110
Contact.Builder class 26
Contact class
  about 25
  contact information, updating 27
  contact objects, creating 26, 27
contactDoesNotExist() method 112
ContactDTO 36
Contact findOne() method 52
contact information
  updating 27
contact objects
  creating 26
ContactPOJOMessageListener class 124
ContactRepository class 50
ContactRepositoryImpl class 34, 81
ContactRepository interface 34
contactSerializer() method 117
ContactService interface 36, 109
contacts table 10
convertAndSend() method 127
create, CRUD functions 37
created query, Querydsl
  executing 59
Criteria API 9, 12
criteria queries
  creating 52
criteria query, JPA Criteria API
  creating 52
CRUD application implementation
  about 107
  data, storing in JSON 117
  default serializers, using 108

CRUD application implementation, by data storage in JSON

about 117
application context, configuring 117
Redis atomic long bean, configuring 118
Redis template bean, configuring 117
value serializer bean, configuring 117

CRUD functions

about 36
create 37
delete 40
implementing 36, 37
read 38
update 39

CRUD functions, default serializers 109-113

CRUD functions implementation

about 24
custom repository, creating 30
domain model 24

CRUD operation 9

CRUD operations, default serializers

create 113
delete 116
read 114, 115
update 115

CRUD operations, for Contact objects in JSON format

about 118-120
create 120
delete 122
read 121
update 122

custom functionality

adding, to all repositories 84
adding, to single repository 78

custom functionality, adding to all repositories

about 84
base repository interface, creating 84
base repository interface, implementing 85
repository factory bean, creating 86
repository interface, creating 88
service layer, implementing 89
Spring Data JPA, configuring 88

custom functionality, adding to single repository

about 78

custom interface, creating 79
custom interface, implementing 79
custom methods, implementing 81, 82
repository class, configuring 80
repository interface, creating 82
service implementation, creating 83

custom interface

creating 79
implementing 79

custom methods

implementing 81

custom repository

creating 30
creating, in old school way 30-34
creating, with Spring Data JPA 35

D

Database 18
dataBase property 97
database queries

creating 9
Criteria API 12
JPQL 11
Native SQL queries 10

data source bean

configuring 21

dataSource() method 21
data structures, Redis

hash 104
list 104
set 104
sorted set 104
string 104

data transfer object (DTO) 36
data types, Redis

about 13
hash 13
list 13
set 13
sorted set 13
string 13

default serializers, used for implementing CRUD application

about 108
application context, configuring 108
CRUD functions, implementing 109

Redis atomic long bean, configuring 109
Redis template bean, configuring 108
deleteById() method 40, 85, 133, 116
delete, CRUD functions 40
dependencies, Spring Data Redis
getting 94
domain model, CRUD
about 24
Address class 28
Contact class 25

E

embedded class 28
entity 9
entity class 9
entity manager 9
entity manager factory 9
entity manager factory bean
configuring 22
entityManagerFactory() method 22
executed query, Querydsl
creating 58

F

findAllForPage() method 70, 81
findAll() method 38, 114
findById() method 38, 115, 121
findContactsForPage() method 82
findOne() method 38
firstOrLastNameStartsWith() method 53, 82

G

GenericToStringSerializer<T>
Serializer 106
getBuilder() method 26
getEntityClass() method 32
getEntityManager() method 32
getId() method 30
getLikePattern() method 53
getRepositoryBaseClass() method 87
getTargetRepository() method 87

H

handleMessage() method 124

hash, data types 104
HashOperations<K,HK,HV> opsForHash()
method 105
hostName property 97

I

incrementAndGet() method 112
installing
Redis 92, 93
int getOffset() method 67
int getPageNumber() method 67
int getPageSize() method 67
isMember() method 112

J

JacksonJsonRedisSerializer<T>
Serializer 106
Java EE application server 8
Java Persistence API. *See* **JPA**
Java Persistence Query
Language (JPQL) 9, 11
JdkSerializationRedisSerializer
Serialize 106
JedisConnectionFactory class
configuration properties 97
Jedis connector
about 95
configuring 97
JPA
about 8
database queries, creating 9
Enterprise JavaBeans (EJB) 8
Hibernate 8
JDBC API 8
key concepts 9
object-relational mapping (ORM)
frameworks 8
JPA Criteria API
about 52
cons 55
criteria query, creating 52
pros 55
query results, paginating 74
service method, creating 54
specifications, creating 53
static metamodel class, creating 53

JPA Criteria API support
  adding, to repository 52
JPA provider 17
JpaRepositoryFactoryBean class 88
JpaSpecificationExecutor<T> interface 52
JPQL queries 62
JRedisConnectionFactory class
  configuration properties 98
JRedis connector
  about 95
  configuring 98, 99

K

key components, Redis
  about 105
  Atomic counters 105
  RedisTemplate 105
keywords 44

L

list<contact> findAll() method 52
list, data types 104
ListOperations<K,V> opsForList()
        method 105
long count() method 52

M

Maven
  dependencies, downloading 17, 18
Maven APT plugin configuration 57
MessageListenerAdapter class 123
messageListenerAdapter() method 125
message listener container 126
MessageListener interface
  implementing 123
message listeners, publish/subscribe
        messaging pattern
  creating 123
  MessageListener interface,
        implementing 123
  POJO message listener, creating 124
method prefixes
  about 42
  findBy 42
  get 42

getBy 42
read 42
readBy 42

N

named query
  cons 49
  creating 46, 48
  pros 49
  query method, creating 48
  service method, creating 48
Native SQL queries 10
notifications, sending with RedisTemplate
  deleted contacts 128
  new contact 127
  updated contacts 127

O

object-relational mismatch 8
onMessage() method 123
operations, RedisTemplate class
  about 105
  methods 105
OxmSerializer Serializer 106

P

PageRequest objects
  creating 69
pagination, implementing
  @Query annotation 72
  JPA Criteria API 74
  JpaRepository 70
  named queries 71
  Querydsl 74
  query generation from method name
        strategy 71
password property 97
persistence context 9
persistence mechanisms
  about 14
  AOF 14
  RDB 14
persistence unit 9
persist() method 112, 113

POJO message listener
  creating 124
poolConfig property 97
port property 97
property expressions
  about 43
  AddressStreetAddress 43
  combining, with keywords 44
  LastName 43
property resolution algorithm
  working 43
pros, JPA Criteria API 55
pros, named query 49
pros, @Query annotation 51
pros, Querydsl 59
pros, query generation from method
      name 46
publish/subscribe messaging pattern
  about 15, 16, 123
  application context, configuring 125
  message listeners, creating 123
  messages, sending with RedisTemplate 127
  wanted behaviour, verifying 128

Q

queries
  building 42
  building, query methods used 42
Querydsl
  about 55
  cons 59
  created query, executing 59
  executed query, creating 58
  pros 59
  Querydsl-Maven integration,
      configuring 56
  Querydsl query type, generating 57
  query results, paginating 74
Querydsl Maven dependencies
  configuring 56
Querydsl-Maven integration
  code generation Maven plugin,
      configuring 56
  configuring 56
  Querydsl Maven dependencies,
      configuring 56

QuerydslPredicateExecutor<T> interface 65
QueryDslPredicateExecutor<T> interface 58
Querydsl query type
  generating 57
Querydsl support
  adding, to repository 58
query generation from method name
      strategy
  about 42
  cons 46
  keywords 44
  method prefixes 42
  property expressions 43
  pros 46
  search function, implementing 45
query method, method name strategy
  creating 61
query method, named query
  creating 48
query method, @Query annotation
  creating 50
query methods
  about 42
  creating 42
  creating, property expressions and
      keywords used 44
  techniques for creating 42
query results
  paginating 67
  sorting 60
  sorting, with method name 61
  sorting, with Querydsl 65
  sorting, with query strings 62
  sorting, with Sort class 62
query results, paginating
  service layer, changing 68
query results pagination, named queries
  pagination support, adding to query
      method 72
  service class, modifying 72
query results pagination, @Query
      annotation
  pagination support, adding to query
      method 73
  service class, modifying 73

query results pagination, query generation
    from method name strategy
  pagination support, adding to query
    method 71
  service class, modifying 71
query results, sorting with method name
  about 61
  query method, creating 61
  service method, modifying 61
query results, sorting with Querydsl 65, 66
query results, sorting with query strings
  about 62
  JPQL queries 62
  SQL queries 62
query results, sorting with Sort class
  @Query annotation 64
  about 62
  JPA Criteria API 65
  JpaRepository 63
  query generation from method name
    strategy 64

R

RDB, persistence mechanisms 14
read, CRUD functions 38
Redis. *See* **Spring Data Redis**
  about 13
  persistence 14
  publish/subscribe messaging pattern 15
  replication 15
  supported data types 13
RedisAtomicInteger 105
RedisAtomicLong 105
redisAtomicLong() method 118
Redis connection
  configuring 95, 96
redisConnectionFactory() method 94, 97, 99,
  131
Redis data model
  designing 104
RedisTemplate 105
RedisTemplate class
  methods 106
  operations 105
  serializers 106
redisTemplate() method 118

replication 15
repository
  JPA Criteria API support, adding 52
  Querydsl support, adding to 58
repository class
  configuring 80
RepositoryContactService class 45, 51, 61
repository factory bean
  builder method, creating 88
  creating 86
  repository factory inner class, creating 86,
    87
  skeleton, creating 86
repository factory inner class
  creating 86
repository interface
  creating 82, 88
resultClass property 47
RjcConnectionFactory class
  configuration properties 100
RJC connector
  about 96
  configuring 99, 100

S

search function
  implementing 45
search() method 45
separation of concerns principle 77
serializers, RedisTemplate class
  about 106, 107
  GenericToStringSerializer<T> 106
  JacksonJsonRedisSerializer<T> 106
  JdkSerializationRedisSerializer 106
  OxmSerializer 106
  StringRedisSerializer 106
service implementation
  creating 83
service layer
  implementing 89
service layer, query results pagination
  changing 68
  class, creating 68
  PageRequest objects, creating 69
  service interface, changing 69

service method, JPA Criteria API
  creating 54
service method, method name strategy
  modifying 61
service method, named query
  creating 48
service method, @Query annotation
  creating 51
set, data types 104
SetOperations<K,V> opsForSet()
    method 105
shardInfo property 97
sortByLastNameAndFirstNameAsc()
    method 69, 81
sortByLastNameAndFirstNameAsc()
    method 66
sorted set, data types 104
Sort getSort() method 67
sorting
  query results 60
  query results, with method name 61
  query results, with Querydsl 65
  query results, with query strings 62
  query results, with Sort class 62
specifications, JPA Criteria API
  creating 53
Spring application context
  application context configuration class,
      creating 20
  configuring 19, 94, 95
  properties file, creating 19
Spring cache abstraction
  cached methods, identifying 132
  configuring 130
  contact information, adding 133
  contact information, deleting 133
  contact information, updating 133
  verifying 134
Spring cache abstraction configuration
  about 130
  cache manager bean, configuring 132
  caching annotations, enabling 130
  host and port, configuring 131
  Redis connection factory bean,
      configuring 131
  Redis template bean, configuring 131

Spring Data JPA
  about 35
  components 17
  configuring 88
  reference manual 44
  used, for creating custom repository 35
Spring Data Redis
  about 91
  CRUD application, implementing 107
  dependencies, getting 94
  installing 92, 93
  key components 105
  publish/subscribe messaging pattern 123
  Spring cache abstraction, using with 129
  URL 91
Spring Data Redis connection configuration
  about 95
  Jedis connector, configuring 97
  JRedis connector, configuring 98, 99
  RJC connector, configuring 99, 100
  SRP connector, configuring 101
Spring Framework 18
SQL queries 62
SrpConnectionFactory class
  configuration properties 101
SRP connector
  about 96
  configuring 101
  URL 96
static metamodel class, JPA Criteria API
  creating 53
String buildKey(Long contactId) method
    110, 119
string, data types 104
String persist(Contact persisted)
    method 110
StringRedisSerializer Serializer 106

T

techniques, for creating query methods
  named queries 46
  Query annotation 49
  query generation from method name 42
  selecting 60
techniques, for sorting query results
  method name, sorting 61

Querydsl, used 65
query strings, sorting 62
selecting 67
Sort class, sorting 62
timeout property 97
toPredicate() method 53
transaction manager bean
configuring 23
transactionManager() method 23

U

update, CRUD functions 39

update() method 39, 115
usePool property 97

V

ValueOperations<K,V> opsForValue()
method 106
void persist(Contact persisted) method 119

Z

ZSetOperations<K,HK,HV> opsForZSet()
method 106

Thank you for buying
Spring Data

About Packt Publishing

Packt, pronounced 'packed', published its first book "*Mastering phpMyAdmin for Effective MySQL Management*" in April 2004 and subsequently continued to specialize in publishing highly focused books on specific technologies and solutions.

Our books and publications share the experiences of your fellow IT professionals in adapting and customizing today's systems, applications, and frameworks. Our solution based books give you the knowledge and power to customize the software and technologies you're using to get the job done. Packt books are more specific and less general than the IT books you have seen in the past. Our unique business model allows us to bring you more focused information, giving you more of what you need to know, and less of what you don't.

Packt is a modern, yet unique publishing company, which focuses on producing quality, cutting-edge books for communities of developers, administrators, and newbies alike. For more information, please visit our website: www.packtpub.com.

About Packt Open Source

In 2010, Packt launched two new brands, Packt Open Source and Packt Enterprise, in order to continue its focus on specialization. This book is part of the Packt Open Source brand, home to books published on software built around Open Source licences, and offering information to anybody from advanced developers to budding web designers. The Open Source brand also runs Packt's Open Source Royalty Scheme, by which Packt gives a royalty to each Open Source project about whose software a book is sold.

Writing for Packt

We welcome all inquiries from people who are interested in authoring. Book proposals should be sent to author@packtpub.com. If your book idea is still at an early stage and you would like to discuss it first before writing a formal book proposal, contact us; one of our commissioning editors will get in touch with you.

We're not just looking for published authors; if you have strong technical skills but no writing experience, our experienced editors can help you develop a writing career, or simply get some additional reward for your expertise.

HBase Administration Cookbook

ISBN: 978-1-84951-714-0   Paperback: 332 pages

Master HBase configuration and administration for optimum database performance

1. Move large amounts of data into HBase and learn how to manage it efficiently

2. Set up HBase on the cloud, get it ready for production, and run it smoothly with high performance

3. Maximize the ability of HBase with the Hadoop eco-system including HDFS, MapReduce, Zookeeper, and Hive

RESTful PHP Web Services

ISBN: 978-1-84719-552-4   Paperback: 220 pages

Learn the basic architectural concepts and steps through examples of consuming and creating RESTful web services in PHP

1. Get familiar with REST principles

2. Learn how to design and implement PHP web services with REST

3. Real-world examples, with services and client PHP code snippets

4. Introduces tools and frameworks that can be used when developing RESTful PHP applications

Please check **www.PacktPub.com** for information on our titles

Spring Web Services 2 Cookbook

ISBN: 978-1-84951-582-5   Paperback: 322 pages

Over 60 recipes providing comprehensive coverage of practical real-life implementation of Spring-WS

1. Create contract-first Web services

2. Explore different frameworks of Object/XML mapping

3. Secure Web Services by Authentication, Encryption/Decryption and Digital Signature

4. Learn contract-last Web Services using Spring Remoting and Apache CXF

5. Implement automated functional and load testing

PHP and MongoDB Web Development Beginner's Guide

ISBN: 978-1-84951-362-3   Paperback: 292 pages

Combine the power of PHP and MangoDB to build dynamic web 2.0 applications

1. Learn to build PHP-powered dynamic web applications using MongoDB as the data backend

2. Handle user sessions, store real-time site analytics, build location-aware web apps, and much more, all using MongoDB and PHP

3. Full of step-by-step instructions and practical examples, along with challenges to test and improve your knowledge

Please check **www.PacktPub.com** for information on our titles

Lightning Source UK Ltd.
Milton Keynes UK
UKOW06f1946220814

237401UK00002B/39/P